Mediterranean Crockpot Cookbook Made Simple

Healthy, Easy, Slow Cooker Recipes. Fix Before Work-Eat When at Home.

Sherri Todd

Copyright @2024 by Sherri Todd

FIRST EDITION

Your Feedback is Greatly Appreciated!

It's through your feedback, support and reviews that I'm able to create the best books possible and serve more people.

I would be extremely grateful if you could take just 60 seconds to kindly leave an honest review of the book on Amazon. Please share your feedback and thoughts for others to see.

To do so, simply find the book on Amazon's website (or wherever you purchased the book from) and locate the section to leave a review. Select a star rating and write a couple of sentences.

That's it! Thank you so much for your support.

Review this product

Share your thoughts with other customers

Write a customer review

Click with your camera above to get a free e-book: "Mediterranean Diet Program: Healthy Effective Weight Loss or copy/type in https://sforbes-publishing-llc-2.ck.page/dabe20d639.

Table of Content

Contents

Introduction

In today's fast-paced and busy world, finding the time to cook wholesome meals can be a constant struggle. Many people end up resorting to unhealthy takeout or ready-made meals simply because they lack the time or inspiration to prepare something nutritious. Moreover, the stress of juggling work, family, and social commitments often leaves us feeling overwhelmed and exhausted.

Many people make the mistake of thinking that eating a healthy diet means settling for boring and bland foods. But this is a common misconception. Truth is, there are actually plenty healthy diet programs out there that allow you to enjoy delicious foods without having to worry about putting your health at risk. One such diet program is the Mediterranean diet.

The diet program involves adopting the eating habits and cooking methods of people from the Mediterranean region. The interest in this diet started all the way back from the 1960s when an expert pointed out that there is lower incidence of heart disease and heart-related deaths in the countries in the Mediterranean region, including Italy and Greece among others when compared to countries in the Northern Europe, and to the United States.

Researchers conducted studies and experiments on the Mediterranean diet and its effects on heart health. Results from these studies confirm that the diet is one of the major reasons that people who reside or originate from these countries are at lower risk of heart disease as well as of other serious ailments. Because of this, the Mediterranean Diet has been recognized by institutions such as the World Health Organization as a healthy diet program.

Alongside Mediterranean diet, is the crock pot which offer a premium cooking experience for busy Mediterranean dieter. Also known as the slow cooker, the crock pot is a cooking device designed to cook food slowly for long hours. The result is a dish that is bursting with so much flavor. Utilising this device is a game-changer when it comes to convenience and time saving. Therefore, if you are a busy professional, a parent juggling multiple responsibilities, who appreciates tasty and healthy meals, Mediterranean crock pot combo is your answer. The Mediterranean slow cooker is one of the biggest healthy cooking combination.

The use of a crock pot dramatically reduces the typical prep and "stove-watching" time associated with many traditional Mediterranean dishes. Where classic sauces, meats, and stews once took a dedicated housewife a full day of preparation time, the pot delivers the same sort of slow-simmered goodness without all the watch time. Simply set the slow cooker and let it do the rest.

The flavors—and health benefits—of Mediterranean cuisine are undeniable and incredibly delicious. When made in the crock pot, they become easier than ever to prepare and enjoy. With the hundreds of simple recipes included in this book, healthy Mediterranean cooking has never been so simple! Set your slow cooker, eat ... and enjoy!

The Mediterranean Diet Overview

 Although nowadays touted as a modern way of eating, Mediterranean cuisine is rooted in traditional practices of the diverse countries bordering the deep, azure sea "between the lands" that gives the cuisine its moniker. The flavorful foods of Greece, Italy, Morocco, Southern France, and Spain readily come to mind as representative of this style of eating, often praised for its inherently healthful aspects. If the idea of cooking and eating Mediterranean dishes seems exotic or difficult to accomplish, don't be the least bit daunted. The basic foods and ingredients needed to stock your Mediterranean kitchen can be easily obtained at most major grocery stores.

The colors and flavors of Mediterranean cuisine signal the broad range of vitamins and other nutrients it provides. This cuisine is generally defined by a very high proportion of fruits, vegetables, legumes, whole grains, and olive oil; a relatively high proportion of seafood; a moderate proportion of dairy products; moderate wine consumption; and proportionately lower amounts of other lean meats.

When meal planning and choosing which recipes to try, aim to include fruits, vegetables, and whole grains in most of your meals. Fruits, vegetables, pasta, beans, and minimally processed whole grains make up the largest proportion of the Mediterranean cuisine and will lend substance and flavor to the Mediterranean-style dishes you prepare in your slow cooker.

Healthful fats are also a major component of this now popular cuisine. Olives and olive oil are staples of Mediterranean cooking; nuts and seeds are also high-quality sources of healthful fats, fiber, and protein. Unprocessed, natural cheeses, yogurt, and milk are an important part of Mediterranean cuisine, although in more modest proportion than, for example, the vegetable, fruit, legume, and whole grain groups.

As for protein, Mediterranean cuisine is full of choices. Fish and shellfish provide excellent protein and healthful fats when following a Mediterranean diet. Eggs offer high-quality protein, particularly for vegetarians. Lean, unprocessed meats are also sources of protein in this style of cooking and eating.

The Mediterranean Diet Origins

The origins of the Mediterranean diet may be traced back to the eating patterns and agricultural methods of the nation's bordering the Mediterranean Sea, including Greece, Italy, Spain, and Morocco. These nations have strong culinary traditions based upon the utilisation of fresh, whole, and locally obtained ingredients such fruits, vegetables, whole grains, olive oil, seafood, and legumes.

The identification of the Mediterranean diet as a distinct dietary pattern emerged from observational studies undertaken in the mid-20th century. In the late 1940s, the American scientist

Ancel Keys began on the historic Seven Countries Study. This study aims to evaluate the association between nutrition, lifestyle, and cardiovascular disease (CVD) in diverse communities around the world. Ancel Keys observed a notable discrepancy in the rates of CVD between populations in Western nations, such as the United States and Finland, and those in Mediterranean countries, such as Greece and Italy. The Mediterranean inhabitants had much lower incidence of heart disease and greater life expectancies.

Upon further research of the dietary patterns in these Mediterranean locations, Keys discovered a consistent dietary pattern defined by high intake of fruits, vegetables, legumes, whole grains, fish, and olive oil, combined with modest consumption of dairy products and red wine. This food pattern stood out as a potential reason for the reduced prevalence of heart disease and overall improved health found in these locations.

Subsequent research undertaken in the following decades began to corroborate the health advantages of the Mediterranean diet. Researchers discovered that adherence to the Mediterranean diet was connected with a decreased risk of many chronic illnesses, including heart disease, stroke, diabetes, certain forms of cancer.

The Science Behind the Mediterranean Diet

The Mediterranean diet is a modern nutritional diet plan inspired by traditional dietary patterns that come from the countries situated surrounding of Mediterranean Sea. The research and studies conducted on the Mediterranean diet show that the diet reduces the risk of cardiovascular diseases. The study conducted over 2600 women over 12 years found a 25% less risk of developing cardiovascular disease.

The 15-year-long research and study on the Mediterranean diet published in JAMA International Medicine found that persons who eat refined carbs have a 38% greater risk of dying from heart-related diseases. According to the American Heart Association, the limit of added sugar in your daily Mediterranean diet is 36 grams for men and 25 grams for women.

Olive oil is used as the main fat during the Mediterranean diet. It is one of the best sources of monounsaturated fats to improve your insulin sensitivity and control your blood sugar level. If you don't have diabetes, it also helps to reduce the risk of developing diabetes. Some of the research and studies also state that women who follow the Mediterranean diet have a lower risk of breast and stomach cancer.

The Mediterranean Diet Food Pyramid

The Mediterranean diet pyramid is a graphic depiction of the recommended dietary categories and amounts in the Mediterranean diet. It gives guidance for anyone wishing to adopt a Mediterranean-style eating pattern.

At the base of the pyramid are physical exercise and social interactions, which are stressed as vital components of general health and well-being. Regular physical exercise, such as walking, riding, or swimming, is recommended, since it is a typical habit in Mediterranean countries. Additionally, the Mediterranean diet encourages mingling and sharing meals with family and friends, since it helps develop a feeling of community and enjoyment surrounding food.

Moving up the pyramid, the following level provides an abundance of plant-based meals. This involves ingesting a variety of fruits, vegetables, whole grains, legumes, nuts, and seeds. These foods are great sources of important vitamins, minerals, fiber, and antioxidants. They should make up a large component of regular meals and should be ingested in its complete, unprocessed forms.

Above the plant-based foods category, the Mediterranean diet advocates utilising extra virgin olive oil as the major source of fat. Olive oil is commonly used in Mediterranean cuisine for cooking, dressing salads, and spreading over foods. It includes monounsaturated fats, antioxidants, and anti-inflammatory qualities, boosting heart health.

Next, moderate consumption of fish, poultry, dairy products, and eggs is suggested. These foods are key providers of lean protein and vital nutrients such as omega-3 fatty acids. Fish, particularly fatty fish like salmon and sardines, are rich in omega-3s, which have been connected with several health advantages, including heart health and cognitive function.

Above this level is the limited eating of red meat. Red meat, including beef, hog, and lamb, should be taken sparingly on the Mediterranean diet due to its increased saturated fat level. Instead, the emphasis should be on lean sources of protein, such as fish and chicken, as discussed before.

Finally, at the summit of the pyramid, sweets and sugary beverages are put. These should be consumed in moderation and maintained to a minimum. While Mediterranean sweets can be eaten sometimes, they are often smaller in quantity size and produced with healthy components such as fresh fruits, almonds, and honey.

It's crucial to note that the Mediterranean diet pyramid also promotes the necessity of water as the main beverage, as well as the occasional moderate use of red wine with meals, largely for its possible cardiovascular advantages. However, moderation is vital, and excessive alcohol intake should be avoided.

What to Eat on the Mediterranean Diet?

The Mediterranean diet is a plant-based diet that promotes eating the natural, seasonable fruits and vegetables found in Mediterranean countries. The diet is rich in fiber, vitamins, minerals, nutrients, and antioxidants. The following food list will help you to choose natural and healthy ingredients during the Mediterranean diet.

Greens: This category includes fresh vegetables. The vegetables are naturally low in calories and fats. They are also rich in fiber, vitamins, nutrients, and antioxidants. It helps to reduce the risk of heart disease, strokes, and digestive problems, and control blood pressure, and blood sugar. The list of greens in the Mediterranean diet includes. Spinach, lettuce, kale, arugula, green turnip, broccoli, beet, green mustard, tomato, olives, bell peppers, garlic, carrot, cauliflower, artichokes, green beans, leafy greens, Brussels, onion, etc.

Whole Grains: are a good source of fiber, vitamin B, minerals, protein, and antioxidants. The Mediterranean diet is rich in whole grains which helps to reduce the risk of heart attack, stroke, type-2 diabetes some form of cancer, obesity, and high blood pressure. The list of whole grains in the Mediterranean diet includes. Barley, couscous, brown rice, pasta, whole oats, quinoa, pasta, ray, corn, whole wheat, orzo, and whole bread grains.

Fruits: are a good source of fiber, vitamins, and minerals. It also comes with an antioxidant-like flavonoid. Eating fruits during the Mediterranean diet will help to reduce the risk of developing diabetes, cancer, inflammation, and heart-related diseases. The list of fruits in the Mediterranean diet includes. Grapes, lemon, tomatoes, oranges, apples, figs, kiwi, watermelon, avocado, peaches, pears, apricots, pomegranate, cherries, olives, tangerines, strawberries, dates, plum, banana, etc.

Nuts and Seeds: are rich in fibers, vitamins, minerals, and proteins. They are also rich in healthy fats like monounsaturated fats. It helps to reduce the risk of heart disease, and diabetes, and control cholesterol levels. The nuts and seeds during the Mediterranean diet include. Almonds, cashews, walnuts, peanuts, pine nuts, pistachios, macadamia nuts, hazelnuts, pumpkin seeds, sesame seeds, sunflower seeds, flax seeds, etc.

Legumes: are a good source of fiber, iron, protein, folate, magnesium, and potassium. It also has antioxidant properties to slow down the aging process prevent cell damage and fight against diseases. Legumes during the Mediterranean diet include. Kidney bean, white bean, pinto bean, black bean, lentils, pulses, chickpeas, peanuts, hummus, etc.

Meat and Poultry: A moderate amount of red meat and poultry is allowed during the Mediterranean diet. Meat and poultry are one of the good sources of protein. Meat and protein during the Mediterranean diet include.: Red meat, goat, lamb, beef, pork, turkey, chicken, goose, duck, etc.

Seafood Fish: is used as an important source of protein and omega-3 fatty acids in the Mediterranean diet. Omega-3 is nothing but polyunsaturated fatty acids which help to reduce inflammation and reduce the risk of strokes and heart failure. The seafood during the Mediterranean diet includes. Sardine, salmon, trout, flounder, mackerel, Pollock, tuna, herring, tilapia, crab, shrimp, lobster mackerel, squid, clams, abalone, octopus, etc.

Healthy fats: Olive oil is used as the main fat in the Mediterranean diet. It is a rich source of monounsaturated fats and antioxidants. Olive oil also has anti-inflammatory properties that protect you from heart disease, weight gain, and obesity. Healthy fats during the Mediterranean diet include: Olive oil, extra-virgin olive oil, grape seed oil, avocado oil, etc.

Food to Avoid

During the Mediterranean diet, it is recommended to avoid highly processed and refined food. The following list of non-approved foods from the Mediterranean diet includes.

Highly Processed Foods: are high in calories and low in nutrients. They contain preservatives that make them high in sugar, salt, carbohydrates, and saturated fats. Avoid such unhealthy foods during the Mediterranean diet. Highly processed foods include. Energy drinks, fizzy drinks, ready meals, white bread, candies, sugary snacks, and highly processed meat like hot dogs, bacon, ham, etc.

Refined Foods: Avoid refined foods, refined grains, and refined oils during the Mediterranean diet because they are low in fiber, proteins, and other essential nutrients. They are responsible for blood sugar spikes. Refined oil is unhealthy they are responsible for increasing triglycerides and bad cholesterol. It causes immune dysfunction, diabetes, and obesity. Refined foods include. Refined grains such as white pasta, white bread, white flour, and pizza dove.

Crock Pot Basics

The slow cooker, commonly known as a Crock Pot, is an indispensable tool in the kitchen, especially when preparing Mediterranean dishes. Its ability to simmer and stew ingredients over an extended period not only enhances flavors but also makes meal preparation more convenient.

Cooking food long, low, and slow is one of the best ways to attain deep, satisfying flavors. Crock pots can be accomplished using dry heat, as in a roaster or the oven, or using moist heat, which is the basis of cooking with an electric slow cooker. As food cooks in a sealed ceramic slow-cooker pot and steam accumulates, the condensation collecting inside the crock acts as an efficient baster, leading to extremely juicy, tender meats, vegetables, and other ingredients.

Using the crock pot is one of the easiest ways to introduce healthy home cooking into even the busiest of lifestyles. You can generally put the desired ingredients in your pot and return hours later or at the end of the day to a delicious, ready-to-eat meal. Even if you've never used them before, you can quickly become a slow cooking pro! And why wouldn't you? There are many benefits to this style of cooking, some of which may even surprise you.

Why are Crock Pots Good for the Mediterranean Diet?

The Mediterranean Diet is renowned for its emphasis on fresh, wholesome ingredients, heart-healthy fats, and a balanced approach to nutrition. When considering the virtues of the Crock Pot in the context of this diet, several factors come into play, making it a remarkably suitable cooking method that aligns well with the principles of Mediterranean cuisine.

Firstly, the Mediterranean Diet places great importance on the consumption of vegetables, legumes, and lean proteins, all of which can be easily incorporated into Crock Pot recipes. The slow-cooking process allows these ingredients to meld together, enhancing their flavors and preserving their nutritional value. Vegetables like tomatoes, bell peppers, zucchini, and eggplant, often staples in Mediterranean cooking, benefit from the slow simmering of a Crock Pot, developing rich, savory profiles that contribute to the overall taste of a dish.

Moreover, the use of olive oil, a cornerstone of the Mediterranean Diet, pairs seamlessly with the Crock Pot's low and slow cooking method. The gentle heat helps infuse the dishes with the distinct fruity and peppery notes of extra virgin olive oil, enhancing the authenticity of Mediterranean flavors. This cooking technique also promotes the breakdown of tougher cuts of meat, turning them tender and succulent, aligning with the diet's preference for lean protein sources like fish and poultry.

In addition to enhancing flavor, the Crock Pot supports the Mediterranean Diet's commitment to convenience and simplicity. The one-pot nature of many Crock Pot recipes streamlines the cooking process, reducing the need for multiple pots and pans.

This not only makes meal preparation more straightforward but also minimizes cleanup, encouraging adherence to the diet by making it more accessible to those with busy lifestyles.

The Crock Pot's gentle and consistent heat is particularly advantageous for Mediterranean dishes that often involve slow-cooking methods. Traditional Mediterranean recipes such as stews, soups, and braised dishes benefit from the Crock Pot's ability to maintain a low, even temperature over an extended period, allowing the flavors to meld harmoniously. This slow infusion of flavors is emblematic of the Mediterranean approach to savoring meals, promoting a more relaxed and enjoyable dining experience.

Furthermore, the Crock Pot's versatility complements the diverse range of ingredients found in the Mediterranean Diet. Whether it's grains, legumes, or an array of vegetables, the Crock Pot accommodates various elements, enabling the creation of hearty and satisfying meals that embody the essence of Mediterranean cuisine. The adaptability of the Crock Pot encourages culinary experimentation, making it easy for individuals to personalize their dishes while still adhering to the principles of the Mediterranean Diet.

Benefits of Slow Cooking

In today's fast-paced world, using a slow cooker lets you economize your time and effort in the kitchen. Often, the first reason people reach for a crock pot is that they are easy to use and they save so much time.

This style of cooking lets you plan ahead and have the option to leave your morning free. If you're short on time in the morning, do your prep work the night before and refrigerate ingredients overnight. This way you can simply assemble the ingredients in the crock pot in the morning, turn it on, and head out the door. Just remember: when you wake up, take the ingredients out of the refrigerator to reach room temperature before cooking.

Using a slow cooker also crock pot is one of the best ways to cook the least expensive cuts of meat, letting you cut costs without sacrificing flavor. Beef brisket, chicken thighs, lamb shoulder, and pork shoulder are all great examples of meats that come out tender, juicy, and flavorful after slow cooking but are difficult to prepare successfully otherwise. You can also use less meat in slow cooker recipes because the long simmering brings out the most of the meaty flavor and lets it infuse the whole dish. This in turn allows you to fortify your dishes with vegetables, pastas, whole grains, and beans, in keeping with Mediterranean tradition, while still maintaining a savory, meaty taste.

Tips for Using Your Crock Pot

One key to getting great results time after time with a slow cooker is preparation. That doesn't mean you need to spend a lot of time up front. Just incorporate a few simple habits into your preparation and cooking routine when following or adapting a recipe for a slow crock pot. The following tips and techniques will help you maximize your results every time. Plus, you'll have fun making picture -perfect dishes that will impress your family and friends.

Use the right tools: Use plastic, rubber, or wooden utensils when stirring foods in your glazed ceramic pot or serving dishes from it. Use a soft sponge to clean the cooker since metal utensils and scouring pads can scratch the surface of the crock.

Cut food evenly: Especially when dealing with denser vegetables that are more difficult to cook through, such as carrots, potatoes, or yams, be sure to cut the food into pieces of about the same size. This will ensure that they cook at a similar rate, so you can avoid mushy pieces and underdone pieces in the same dish.

Brown food first as needed: At times—when you are able or when the recipe specifically calls for it—you will want to brown certain foods first to enhance flavor. Onions browned beforehand have a different flavor from those put into the crock pots raw. You may want to experiment, as you might find you prefer one or the other in different recipes. You also may prefer to brown meat for some recipes to give it color and flavor, but generally this is not essential. If you do choose to brown meat or poultry in advance for your recipe, do so by placing a small amount of olive oil in a non-stick skillet large enough to accommodate the meat or poultry. Warm the oil over medium-high heat on the stove until shimmering, and brown the meat or poultry evenly on all sides, in small batches if necessary.

Don't use frozen foods: To maintain food safety, your slow cooker must reach a temperature of at least 140°F in 4 hours or less. A prolonged cooking process at inadequate temperatures increases the likelihood that harmful bacteria will grow in your food. Always thaw frozen vegetables, as directed, and before you add them to the slow cooker. Take special care with larger pieces of meat and poultry, which should be thawed in the refrigerator a day or two before cooking.

Go easy on the liquid: Because your crock pot will have a tightly sealed lid, little or no evaporation occurs during cooking, and this cooking method releases the juices from the other ingredients. Use only enough liquid to make the recipe work. The liquid should just cover the other ingredients. Be careful not to overfill your slow cooker, or liquid might leak out of the top. This will not only make a mess but will prevent the food from cooking as it should. Ideally, your slow cooker should be one-half to two-thirds full and no more than three-quarters full. If adapting a recipe that wasn't written for slow cookers, reduce the liquid by about one-third. And use the liquid to its full advantage: Rather than water, opt for flavorful liquids like fruit juice, chicken stock, seafood stock, vegetable juice, vegetable stock, and wine. Since the liquid won't evaporate, a little will go a long way.

Use fats sparingly: One of the best things about using a slow cooker is that you can really cut down on the amount of fat in your dishes. The moisture inside the sealed crock prevents foods from sticking to the inside of the crock, so you don't need to add oil for that purpose to any of your recipes. Cooking meat on the stove top causes the fat to drain away, but it can't drain out of a slow cooker. Too much fat will result in an unpleasant texture in the final meal, so keep fat to a minimum or eliminate it entirely. Remove skin from chicken and trim excess fat from meat. The flavor of your food won't suffer. And, of course, it goes without saying that less fat means more healthful results.

Keep the lid closed during cooking: Your slow cooker relies upon the tight seal of the lid to help maintain its steam-condensation cycle. When adding ingredients, or if you must check on your food or stir it, do it quickly. Each time you lift off the lid, heat and moisture escape from your slow cooker, and it can take up to 20 minutes to recover the full amount of heat lost. This makes the cooking take longer, and your existing time cycle may not be sufficient.

Choose the right temperature setting: The cooker has two temperature settings: low and high. Low is 200°F and high is 300°F. Both settings cook meat safely. Since food becomes more flavorful the longer it simmers in its own juices, choose the low setting whenever possible for the best taste. This is also the best setting if you plug it in before you go off to work. You won't have to give the slow cooker another thought during your busy day. Choose the high setting when you want a meal in a few hours, rather than at the end of the day. The food will still be delicious, just not quite as flavorful as after an all-day simmer. It's useful to remember that 1 hour on high is equal to about 2½ hours on low. The handy chart at the end of this chapter can help you navigate between the high and low settings to suit your schedule. If a recipe suggests cooking your stew on low for 7 hours, but you want to eat it in 3 hours, just set the slow cooker on high.

Avoid using your crock for food storage: Even when you prep ingredients the night before, store them in a different container. Refrigerating and/or freezing the crock (and then returning it to room temperature and heating it) can cause it to crack. Slow cookers are not intended for reheating food. Use your crock pot to make mouthwateringly good meals; use your oven, stove, toaster oven, or microwave to reheat leftovers—if there are any.

Safety Management:

When using a Crock pot, it's important to remember a few facts about temperature and bacteria. Your Pof must reach a temperature of at least 140°F in 4 hours or less, which is essential to the maintenance of food safety. Any prolonged cooking process at inadequate temperatures increases the risk of harmful bacteria breeding in your food. For these reasons, power outages should be treated with care. If your power was out for under 2 hours, you may resume cooking. Your alternative is to remove the ingredients from the crock and finish cooking using a more conventional method, such as the stove top or oven. If the outage was 2 hours or longer, the food must be discarded to avoid food-borne illnesses.

You already know that pre-browning can have aesthetic and savory value, but browning ingredients before they go into the cooker also has a food-safety benefit. The danger zone for growth of harmful bacteria is between 40°F and 140°F. This means if the food has been warmer than refrigerator temperature but cooler than very hot tap water temperature for too long, it is in danger of becoming a breeding ground for bacteria. By browning meats in advance, you kill any bacteria on the surface of the food. Then once the slow cooking process begins and proceeds, the cooking process eliminates any remaining bacteria.

A final note on extreme temperatures and the ceramic cooking crock and glass lid (if the lid isn't plastic): These parts of a slow cooker can crack or break as they react to dramatic changes in temperature. If very cold ingredients are added when these parts are very hot, or if the parts are placed on very cold surfaces, they may break. Slow cooking is not only easy, but safe, as long as you are mindful of these simple precautionary measures. Always use common sense, and err on the side of caution if you are in doubt.

Breakfast

Egg and Vegetable Breakfast Casserole

Ingredients: *(Time: 4 hours 15 minutes)*

- 8 eggs

- 4 egg whites
- ¾ cup milk (can use almond)
- 2 teaspoons stone ground mustard
- ½ teaspoon garlic salt
- 1 teaspoon salt
- ½ teaspoon pepper
- 1 30-ounce bag frozen hash browns
- 4 strips cooked bacon (optional)
- ½ onion, roughly chopped
- 2 bell peppers, roughly chopped
- 1 small head of broccoli, roughly chopped
- 6 ounces' cheddar cheese

Method: *(Servings: 8)*

1. Mix together the eggs, egg whites, milk, mustard, garlic salt, salt, and pepper until well combined.
2. Spray the inside of the slow cooker with olive oil.
3. Spread half of the bag of hash browns across the bottom of the slow cooker and then top with bacon.
4. Pour egg mixture over the bacon and potatoes.
5. Add the onion, bell peppers and broccoli, then top with remaining hash browns and cheese. Cook on low for 4 hours.

Per serving:

Calories 320, fat 13 g, carbs 29 g, protein 22 g

Berries Oatmeal

Ingredients: *(Time: 6 hours 10 minutes)*

- 1 cup old fashioned oats
- 3 cups almond milk
- 1 cup blackberries
- ½ cup Greek yogurt
- ½ teaspoon cinnamon powder
- ½ teaspoon vanilla extract

Method: *(Servings: 3)*

1. In your slow cooker, mix the oats with the milk, berries, and the other ingredients, toss, put the lid on and cook on Low for 6 hours.
2. Divide into bowls and serve for breakfast.

Per serving:

Calories 356, fat 7.8g, carbs 57.8g, protein 11.7g

Greek Breakfast Casserole

Ingredients: *(Time: 4 hours 10 minutes)*

- Cooking spray
- 12 eggs, beaten

- 1 tablespoon dried onion, chopped
- 1 teaspoon dried garlic, minced
- ½ cup sun-dried tomatoes
- 1 cup mushrooms, sliced
- 2 cups spinach

- ½ cup milk

- Salt and pepper to taste
- ½ cup feta cheese, crumbled

Method: *(Servings: 6)*

1. Spray the slow cooker with oil.
2. Stir everything except the feta cheese in the slow cooker.
3. Sprinkle the feta cheese on top.
4. Seal the pot. Cook on low for 4 hours.

Per serving:

Calories 178 Fat 11.9g, Carbs 3.8g, Protein 14.4g

Breakfast Stuffed Peppers

Ingredients: *(Time: 4 hours 10 minutes)*

- ½ pound ground breakfast sausage
- 4 bell peppers
- 6 large eggs
- 4 ounces Monterey Jack Cheese, shredded
- 4 ounces' fire-roasted chopped green chilies
- ¼ teaspoon salt
- ⅛ teaspoon pepper

Method: *(Servings: 4)*

1. Wash the peppers, cut off the tops and clean out the seeds. Brown the sausage in a skillet.
2. You can use turkey or chicken sausage too, but you need to add a tablespoon of oil to the pan if you do.
3. In a mixing bowl, whisk your eggs until fluffy.

4. Then mix in the cheese and green chilies. Season the egg mixture with salt and pepper.
5. Spray the slow cooker with olive oil and place the peppers inside.
6. Fill each pepper to the top with the egg mixture.
7. Set the slow cooker to high and cook for 2 hours, or cook on low for 4 hours. Serve when egg mixture is set.

Per serving:

Calories 261, fat 16.8 g, carbs 9.2 g, protein 17.3 g

Slow Cooker Frittata

Ingredients: (Time: 2 hours 30minutes)

- 1 (14-ounce) can small artichoke hearts, drained and cut into bite-sized pieces
- 1 (12-ounce) jar roasted red peppers, drained and cut into bite-sized pieces
- ¼ cup sliced green onions
- 8 eggs, beaten
- 4 ounces crumbled Feta cheese
- 1 teaspoon seasoning salt
- ½ teaspoon pepper
- ¼ cup chopped cilantro

Method: (Servings: 6)

1. Spray the slow cooker with olive oil and add the artichoke hearts, red peppers, and green onions.
2. Pour the beaten eggs over the top of the vegetables and stir to combine.
3. Season the mixture with pepper and seasoning salt. Mix in the chopped cilantro.
4. Top with Feta cheese. Cook on low for 2 –3 hours or until set.

Per serving:

Calories 243, fat 14.5 g, carbs 12.7g, protein 15.4 g

Sausage & Hash Brown Casserole

Ingredients: *(Time: 4 hours 25 minutes)*

- 16 oz. pork sausage
- Cooking spray
- 1 lb. hash browns, diced
- 1 onion, diced
- 1 red bell pepper, diced
- 1 green bell pepper, diced
- 2 cups cheddar cheese, shredded
- 12 eggs
- ¼ cup milk
- Salt and pepper to taste

Method: *(Servings: 6)*

1. In a pan over medium heat, cook the sausage until brown.
2. Crumble the sausage, drain the fat and set aside.
3. Spray your slow cooker with oil. Arrange the hash browns, bell peppers, sausage and cheese in layers inside the pot.
4. In a bowl, beat the eggs and stir in the milk. Season with the salt and pepper.
5. Pour egg mixture over the layers. Cover the pot and cook on high for 4 hours.

Per serving:

Calories 135, fat 9g, carbs 1 g, protein 11 g

Cranberry Apple Oatmeal

Ingredients: *(Time: 4-6 hours 5 minutes)*

- 4 cups water
- 2 cups old-fashioned oats
- ½ cup dried cranberries
- 2 apples, peeled and diced
- ¼ cup brown sugar
- 2 tablespoons butter, melted
- ½ teaspoon salt
- 1 teaspoon cinnamon

Method: *(Servings: 4)*

1. Spray your slow cooker with nonstick cooking spray.
2. Add all of the ingredients to the slow cooker and stir to combine.
3. Cook on low for 3 hours. If you want to prepare this the night before, you can cook it up to 6 hours or so.
4. The consistency of the oats will be different if cooked overnight, but it will still be delicious.

Per serving:

Calories 254, fat 7.2 g, carbs 40.9 g, protein 6.4 g

Mediterranean Frittata

Ingredients: *(Time: 3 hours 40 minutes)*

- Cooking spray

- 3 sun-dried tomatoes
- 1 bowl water
- 1 teaspoon olive oil
- ¼ onion, minced
- 4 cloves garlic, minced
- 5 oz. mushrooms, sliced

- ½ cup spinach, chopped
- 6 egg whites
- ¼ cup milk
- ¼ teaspoon dried basil
- Salt and pepper to taste
- 3 oz. feta cheese, crumbled
- 2 tablespoons Parmesan cheese, grated

Method: *(Servings: 4)*

1. Spray your slow cooker with oil. Soak the sun-dried tomatoes in a bowl of water for 10 minutes.
2. Drain and slice into smaller pieces. Pour the oil in a pan over medium heat. Cook the onion and garlic for 5 minutes.
3. Add the mushrooms, spinach and sun-dried tomatoes. Cook for another 5 minutes.
4. In a bowl, beat the eggs white and stir in the milk, basil, salt and pepper. Stir in the mixture from the pan.
5. Add this to the slow cooker. Top with the feta cheese. Seal the pot.
6. Cook on low for 3 hours. Sprinkle the Parmesan cheese on top before serving.

Per serving:

Calories 176, fat 6.2 g, carbs 18.3 g, protein 16.1 g

Blueberry Banana Steel Cut Oats

Ingredients: *(Time: 5-8 hours 5 minutes)*

- 1 cup steel cut oats
- 2 ripe bananas, sliced or mashed
- 1–2 cups fresh or frozen blueberries
- 2 cups water

- 2 cups milk (almond milk works very well in this recipe)
- 2 tablespoons honey or pure maple syrup
- ¼ teaspoon salt
- 1 teaspoon cinnamon
- 2 teaspoons vanilla

Optional add-ins:

- chopped nuts, nut butter, fresh or dried fruit, granola, shredded coconut, honey, additional milk

Method: (Servings: 4)

1. Spray your slow cooker with nonstick cooking spray.
2. Add all the ingredients to the slow cooker and mix well.
3. Cook on low overnight for 6 –8 hours or cook on high for 2 –3 hours.

Per serving:

Calories 297, fat 4.4 g, carbs 58 g, protein 8 g

Berry Breakfast Quinoa

Ingredients: (Time: 2-3 hours 5 minutes)

- 1 large avocado, pitted and smashed
- 4 cups water
- 2 cups quinoa, rinsed
- 2 cups fresh or frozen mixed berries
- 2 tablespoons pure maple syrup
- 2 teaspoons vanilla
- 1 teaspoon cinnamon
- ¼ teaspoon salt

Method: (Servings: 8)

1. Spray your slow cooker with non-stick cooking spray.
2. Add all the ingredients to the slow cooker and mix well.
3. Cook on low for 5 hours or high for 2 –3 hours.

Per serving:

Calories 229, fat 2.8 g, carbs 44 g, protein 7 g

Breakfast Spanish Tortilla

Ingredients: (Time: 3-4 hours 6 minutes)

- 3 tablespoons olive oil
- 2 small onions, peeled and finely diced
- 10 large eggs
- 1 teaspoon kosher salt
- 1 teaspoon ground black pepper
- 4 teaspoons butter, melted
- Non-stick olive oil cooking spray
- 3 large baking potatoes, peeled and thinly sliced

Method: (Servings: 6)

1. Heat olive oil in a skillet over medium heat. Slowly cook onions in olive oil until lightly brown and caramelized, about 5 6 minutes.
2. In a large bowl, whisk together the eggs, salt, and pepper. Grease a 4- to 5-quart slow cooker with melted butter and a spritz of non-stick cooking spray and place half the potatoes on the bottom in a thin layer.
3. Pour half the eggs over the potato layer. Repeat layers, adding onions, ending with the last of the whisked eggs.
4. Cover and cook on high for 3 1/2–4 hours.

Per serving:

Calories: 367, fat: 18g, carbs: 36g, protein: 15g

Potato Frittata with Cheese and Herbs

Ingredients: *(Time: 4 hours)*

- 1 large Yukon gold potato, peeled
- 4 teaspoons butter, melted
- Non-stick olive oil cooking spray
- 6 large eggs
- ½ cup grated Parmesan cheese
- 6 sage leaves, minced
- ½ teaspoon kosher salt
- ½ teaspoon ground black pepper

Method: *(Servings: 4)*

1. Using a mandoline, slice the potato as thinly as possible.
2. Grease a 4- to 5-quart slow cooker with melted butter and a spritz of non-stick cooking spray and place the potatoes on the bottom in a thin layer.
3. In a medium bowl, beat the eggs well. Add the cheese, sage, salt, and pepper; stir to combine.
4. Pour over the potatoes. Cover and cook on high for 2 hours or on low for 4 hours.
5. Cut into squares and serve at once.

Per serving:

Calories: 290, fat: 18g, carbs: 16g, protein: 16g

Ricotta and Parmesan Pancake

Ingredients: *(Time: 2-3 hours)*

- ¾ cup all-purpose flour
- 1 tablespoon baking powder
- 2 large eggs
- 2/3 cup whole milk
- ½ teaspoon kosher salt
- ½ teaspoon freshly ground black pepper
- 1 cup ricotta cheese
- ½ cup Parmesan cheese
- 1 teaspoon olive oil

Method: (Servings: 4)

1. Whisk together the flour, baking powder, eggs, and milk in a medium bowl.
2. Season with salt and pepper. Add the ricotta and Parmesan to the egg mixture and stir well.
3. Grease a 4- to 5-quart slow cooker with olive oil.
4. Pour the ricotta mixture into the slow cooker and cook on high for 2 -3 hours.
5. The pancake is done when a knife in the center comes out clean.
6. Cut into wedges and serve immediately.

Per serving:

Calories: 279, fat: 14g, carbs: 23g, protein: 15g

Rosemary and Pancetta Polenta

Ingredients: (Time: 3-4 hours 10 minutes)

- 2 cups polenta (not quick cooking) or corn meal
- 7 cups hot water
- 2 tablespoons olive oil
- 1 ½ teaspoons kosher salt
- 1 teaspoon freshly ground black pepper

- 2 teaspoons chopped fresh rosemary
- 1 cup shredded Parmesan cheese
- 6 pieces' pancetta, diced into 1" pieces

Method: (Servings: 4)

1. Whisk together the polenta, hot water, olive oil, salt, pepper, and rosemary in a 4- to 5-quart slow cooker. Stir well.
2. Gently whisk in Parmesan. Cook on low for 3 –4 hours or on high for 2 hours. The mixture should be smooth and without any clumps.
3. Preheat oven to 400°F.
4. Line a baking sheet with parchment. Place pancetta on parchment paper and bake for 5–10 minutes or until crispy.
5. Drain on paper towels. Serve polenta garnished with crispy pancetta.

Per serving:

Calories: 616, fat: 34g, carbs: 56g, protein: 19g

Panzanella Strata

Ingredients: (Time: 4 hours)

- 8 large eggs
- 2 cups skim milk

- 1 teaspoon kosher salt
- 1 teaspoon freshly ground black pepper
- ½ cup finely diced red onion
- 1 teaspoon olive oil
- 1 day-old baguette, cut into 1" cubes
- 1½ cups cherry tomatoes, halved
- ½ cup chopped fresh basil

Method: *(Servings: 4)*

1. In a large bowl, whisk together the eggs and milk. Stir in salt, pepper, and onion.
2. Grease a 4- to 5-quart slow cooker with olive oil.
3. Combine the baguette cubes and tomatoes in the slow cooker.
4. Pour the egg mixture over the tomatoes and bread.
5. Cook on low for 4 hours and serve the strata topped with fresh basil.

Per serving:

Calories: 224, fat: 12g, carbs: 11g, protein: 17g

Egg, Tomato, and Pesto Breakfast Bruschetta

Ingredients: (Time: 2 hours 20 minutes)

- 1 ½ teaspoons plus 1 tablespoon olive oil, divided
- 8 large eggs
- 1 teaspoon kosher salt
- 1 teaspoon freshly ground black pepper
- 1 large tomato, diced into ½" pieces
- 1 teaspoon coarse sea salt, crushed
- ½ loaf of Italian or French bread, cut into 4 slices
- ¼ cup pesto
- 1 roasted red pepper, diced
- ½ cup shredded mozzarella cheese

Method: (Servings: 4)

1. Grease a 4- to 5-quart slow cooker with 1 ½ teaspoons olive oil.
2. In a large bowl, whisk eggs, kosher salt, and pepper together until frothy. Pour into slow cooker and cook on low for 1 hour.
3. Break eggs apart and cook on low for an additional hour. Place tomato pieces on a plate and season with sea salt. Let sit for 15 minutes and blot dry with towel.

4. While tomatoes are resting, preheat a grill. Brush bread slices with remaining olive oil. Grill for 3 minutes. Flip and grill for 3 more minutes.
5. Spread pesto on each slice of grilled bread. Stir tomatoes, peppers, and mozzarella into cooked eggs in the slow cooker.
6. Divide egg mixture between grilled bread slices. Serve immediately.

Per serving:

Calories: 464, fat: 34g, carbs: 20g, protein: 20g

Almond and Dried Cherry Granola

Ingredients: (Time: 5 hours)

- 5 cups old-fashioned rolled oats
- 1 cup slivered almonds
- ¼ cup mild honey
- ¼ cup canola oil
- 1 teaspoon vanilla
- ½ cup dried tart cherries
- ¼ cup unsweetened flaked coconut
- ½ cup sunflower seeds

Method: (Servings: 24)

1. Place the oats and almonds in a 4- to 5-quart slow cooker.
2. Drizzle with honey, oil, and vanilla. Stir the mixture to distribute the syrup evenly.
3. Cook on high, uncovered, for 1 1/2 hours, stirring every 15–20 minutes.
4. Add the cherries, coconut, and sunflower seeds.
5. Reduce heat to low. Cook for 4 hours, uncovered, stirring every 20 minutes.
6. Allow the granola to cool fully, and then store it in an airtight container for up to 1 month.

Per serving:

Calories: 140, fat: 7g, protein: 4g, carbs: 16g

Overnight Spiced Cranberry Quinoa

Ingredients: *(Time: 1 ½-2 hours)*

- 1 cup uncooked quinoa
- 2 cups unsweetened almond milk
- 1 tablespoon pumpkin pie spice
- ½ teaspoon vanilla
- Juice and zest of 1 lemon
- 2 tablespoons agave or pure maple syrup
- ½ cup fresh cranberries

Method: *(Servings: 4)*

1. In a medium bowl, rinse quinoa in water. Drain.
2. Place quinoa in a small (1 1/2 - to 3-quart) slow cooker with almond milk, pumpkin pie spice, vanilla, lemon juice and zest, syrup, and cranberries.
3. Cover and cook for 1 ½-2 hours.
4. If the cereal begins to get overly thick and clumpy, add an extra 2 –3 tablespoons of almond milk or water to the slow cooker.

5. Once the quinoa has expanded in size and is tender, use a fork to fluff the cereal.
6. Spoon into a bowl and enjoy!

Per serving:

Calories: 267, fat: 5g, carbs: 47g, protein: 10g

Strawberry Pancake with Roasted Blueberry-Mint Sauce

Ingredients: *(Time: 1 ½-2 hours 25 minutes)*

- ¾ cup all-purpose flour
- 1 tablespoon baking powder
- 1 tablespoon sugar, divided
- 2 large eggs
- 2/3 cup whole milk
- 1 cup diced fresh (or frozen and thawed) strawberries
- 1 tablespoon plus 1 teaspoon olive oil, divided
- 1 ½ cups whole fresh (or frozen and thawed) blueberries
- 1 tablespoon chopped fresh mint

Method: (Servings: 4)

1. Whisk together the flour, baking powder, sugar, eggs, and milk in a medium bowl. Add the strawberries and stir well to combine.
2. Grease the inside of a 4- to 5-quart slow cooker with 1 teaspoon of olive oil.
3. Pour the pancake batter inside the slow cooker and cook on high for 1 ½-2 hours.
4. Preheat oven to 350°F. Place the blueberries in a small (7" × 11"), rimmed baking pan with 1 tablespoon of olive oil.
5. Bake for 20–25 minutes or until blueberries implode. Remove from oven, pour blueberries into a small bowl, and stir in mint.
6. Cut the pancake into wedges and serve with blueberry sauce. Serve immediately.

Per serving:

Calories: 248, fat: 9g, protein: 7.5g, carbs: 35g

Savory French Toast with Herb Purée

Ingredients: (Time: 2-6 hours)

- 6 large eggs
- 3 ½ cups whole milk
- 1 ½ teaspoons kosher salt, divided

- 2 teaspoons freshly ground black pepper, divided
- 3 tablespoons plus
- 1 teaspoon olive oil, divided
- 1 (16-ounce) loaf of day-old Italian bread, cut into 2" cubes
- 1/2 cup flat-leaf parsley
- 2 tablespoons fresh thyme
- 1 tablespoon lemon juice

Method: (Servings: 4)

1. Whisk together the eggs, milk, 1 teaspoon salt, and 1½ teaspoons pepper.
2. Grease the inside of a 4- to 5-quart slow cooker with a teaspoon of olive oil.
3. Place the bread in the bottom of the slow cooker and pour the egg mixture over it.
4. Cook on low for 4-6 hours or on high for 2-3 hours.
5. Place the parsley, thyme, 3 tablespoons of olive oil, ½ teaspoon salt, ½ teaspoon pepper, and lemon juice in a blender.
6. Process until smooth. Reserve. Serve French toast immediately with herb purée.

Per serving:

Calories: 670, Fat: 28g, Carbs: 75g, Protein: 29g

Soup & Stew

Mediterranean Vegetable Soup

Ingredients: *(Time: 6-8 hours 20 minutes)*

- 1 (28-ounce) can no-salt-added diced tomatoes
- 2 cups low-sodium vegetable broth
- 1 green bell pepper, seeded and chopped
- 1 red or yellow bell pepper, seeded and chopped
- 4 ounces' mushrooms, sliced
- 2 zucchinis, chopped
- 1 small red onion, chopped
- 3 garlic cloves, minced
- 1 tablespoon extra-virgin olive oil
- 2 teaspoons dried oregano
- 1 teaspoon paprika
- 1 teaspoon sea salt
- ½ teaspoon freshly ground black pepper
- Juice of 1 lemon

Method: *(Servings: 6)*

1. In a slow cooker, combine the tomatoes, vegetable broth, green and red bell peppers, mushrooms, zucchini, onion, garlic, olive oil, oregano, paprika, salt, and black pepper. Stir to mix well.
2. Cover the cooker and cook for 6 to 8 hours on Low heat. 3.Stir in the lemon juice before serving.

Per serving:

Calories: 91; fat: 3g; carbs: 16g; protein: 3g

Herbed Salmon and Kale Soup

Ingredients: *(Time: 3-5 hours)*

- 2 pounds' fresh salmon fillets, cut into 2-inch pieces
- 1 cup chopped kale
- 3 cups low-sodium vegetable broth or low-sodium chicken broth
- 4 cups water
- 1 small onion, diced
- ½ cup diced carrot
- 2 garlic cloves, minced
- 1 teaspoon dried parsley
- 1 teaspoon dried oregano
- 1 teaspoon dried thyme
- 1 teaspoon sea salt
- ¼ teaspoon freshly ground black pepper

Method: *(Servings: 6)*

1. In a slow cooker, combine the salmon, kale, vegetable broth, water, onion, carrot, garlic, parsley, oregano, thyme, salt, and pepper. Stir to mix well.
2. Cover the cooker and cook for 3 to 5 hours on Low heat.
3. If you do not like salmon, substitute a different fish such as trout or arctic char.

Per serving:

Calories: 212; fat: 6g; Carbs: 6g; Protein: 32g

Lentil Soup

Ingredients: *(Time: 6-8 hours)*

- 1 cup dried red or green lentils
- 4 cups low-sodium vegetable broth

- 4 cups water
- 1 small onion, diced
- 2 carrots, diced
- 2 celery stalks, diced
- 1 cup fresh spinach, chopped
- 1 teaspoon dried oregano
- 1 teaspoon ground cumin
- 1 teaspoon paprika
- 1 teaspoon sea salt, plus more as needed
- ¼ teaspoon freshly ground black pepper, plus more as needed
- Juice of 1 lemon

Method: *(Servings: 6)*

1. In a slow cooker, combine the lentils, vegetable broth, water, onion, carrots, celery, spinach, oregano, cumin, paprika, salt, and pepper. Stir to mix well.
2. Cover the cooker and cook for 6 to 8 hours on Low heat.
3. Stir in the lemon juice. Taste and add more seasoning, if needed, before serving.

Per serving:

Calories: 130; fat: 1g; Carbs: 23g; protein: 9g

Lemon Chicken Soup with Orzo

Ingredients: *(Time: 6-8 hours 10 minutes)*

- 1 pound boneless, skinless chicken thighs
- 4 cups low-sodium chicken broth
- 2 cups water
- 2 celery stalks, thinly sliced
- 1 small onion, diced
- 1 carrot, diced

- 1 garlic clove, minced
- Grated zest of 1 lemon
- Juice of 1 lemon 1 bay leaf
- 1 teaspoon sea salt
- 1 teaspoon dried oregano
- ½ teaspoon freshly ground black pepper
- ¾ cup dried orzo pasta
- 1 lemon, thinly sliced

Method: (Servings: 6)

1. In a slow cooker, combine the chicken, chicken broth, water, celery, onion, carrot, garlic, lemon zest, lemon juice, bay leaf, salt, oregano, and pepper. Stir to mix well.
2. Cover the cooker and cook for 6 to 8 hours on Low heat.
3. Remove the chicken from the slow cooker and shred it.
4. Return the chicken to the slow cooker and add the orzo and lemon slices.
5. Replace the cover on the cooker and cook for 15 to 30 minutes on Low heat, or until the orzo is tender.
6. Remove and discard the bay leaf before serving.

Per serving:

Calories: 195; fat: 5g; Carbs: 22g; protein: 15g

Cream of Zucchini Soup

Ingredients: (Time: 6-8 hours 10 minutes)

- 4 zucchinis, cut into ½-inch chunks
- 4 cups low-sodium vegetable broth
- 1 small onion, diced
- 1 garlic clove, minced
- 1 teaspoon sea salt

- ¼ teaspoon freshly ground black pepper
- ¼ teaspoon dried thyme
- ¼ teaspoon dried rosemary
- ¼ teaspoon dried basil
- ½ cup plain Greek yogurt

Method: *(Servings: 6)*

1. In a slow cooker, combine the zucchini, vegetable broth, onion, garlic, salt, pepper, thyme, rosemary, and basil. Stir to mix well.
2. Cover the cooker and cook for 6 to 8 hours on Low heat. Stir in the yogurt.
3. Using an immersion blender, purée the soup until smooth. Or, transfer the soup to a standard blender, working in batches as needed, and blend until smooth.
4. Use your favorite creamy thickener instead of yogurt such as heavy (whipping) cream, half-and-half, or even coconut milk.

Per serving:

Calories: 55; fat: 2g; Carbs: 9g; protein: 3g

Greek Salad Soup

Ingredients: *(Time: 6-8 hours 15 minutes)*

- 4 tomatoes, cut into wedges
- 2 cucumbers, cut into 1-inch-thick rounds
- 2 green bell peppers, seeded and diced
- 1 small red onion, diced
- 1 cup whole Kalamata olives, pitted
- 4 cups low-sodium chicken broth
- 2 cups water
- 1 tablespoon extra-virgin olive oil
- 2 teaspoons red wine vinegar

- 1½ teaspoons dried oregano
- 1 teaspoon sea salt
- ½ teaspoon freshly ground black pepper
- 4 ounces' feta cheese, crumbled

Method: (Servings: 6)

1. In a slow cooker, combine the tomatoes, cucumbers, bell peppers, onion, olives, chicken broth, water, olive oil, vinegar, oregano, salt, and black pepper. Stir to mix well.
2. Cover the cooker and cook for 6 to 8 hours on Low heat.
3. Top each bowl with feta cheese before serving.

Per serving:

Calories: 180; fat: 12g; Carbs: 13g; protein: 6g

White Bean Soup

Ingredients: (Time: 6-8 hours 10 minutes)

- 1 pound dried white beans, rinsed
- 4 cups water
- 1 (15-ounce) can no-salt-added diced tomatoes
- 2 celery stalks, diced
- 1 cup diced carrot
- 1 small onion, diced
- 2 garlic cloves, minced
- 1 teaspoon dried parsley
- 1 teaspoon dried thyme
- 1 teaspoon sea salt
- ½ teaspoon freshly ground black pepper
- 2 bay leaves

1. In a slow cooker, combine the beans, water, tomatoes, celery, carrot, onion, garlic, parsley, thyme, salt, pepper, and bay leaves. Stir to mix well.
2. Cover the cooker and cook for 6 to 8 hours on Low heat.
3. Remove and discard the bay leaves before serving.

Per serving:

Calories: 282; fat: 1g; Carbs: 53g; Protein: 19g

Minced Beef or Lamb Soup

Ingredients: *(Time: 6-8 hours 20 minutes)*

- 1-pound raw ground beef or lamb
- 12 ounces new red potatoes, halved
- 4 cups low-sodium beef broth
- 2 cups water
- 2 carrots, diced
- 2 celery stalks, diced
- 2 zucchinis, cut into 1-inch pieces
- 1 large tomato, chopped
- 1 small onion, diced
- 2 garlic cloves, minced
- ¼ cup no-salt-added tomato paste
- 1 teaspoon sea salt
- 1 teaspoon dried oregano
- 1 teaspoon dried basil
- ½ teaspoon freshly ground black pepper
- ½ teaspoon dried thyme
- 2 bay leaves

Method: *(Servings: 6)*

1. In a large skillet over medium-high heat, cook the ground meat for 3 to 5 minutes, stirring and breaking it up with a spoon until it has browned and is no longer pink. Drain any grease and put the meat in a slow cooker.
2. Add the potatoes, beef broth, water, carrots, celery, zucchini, tomato, onion, garlic, tomato paste, salt, oregano, basil, pepper, thyme, and bay leaves to the ground meat. Stir to mix well.
3. Cover the cooker and cook for 6 to 8 hours on Low heat. 4.Remove and discard the bay leaves before serving.

Per serving:

Calories: 200; fat: 6g; Carbs: 20g; Protein: 20g

Brussels Sprouts Soup

Ingredients: *(Time: 8 hours 5 minutes)*

- 1 lb fresh brussels sprouts, halved
- 7 oz. fresh baby spinach, torn
- 1 tsp of sea salt
- 1 cup of whole milk
- 3 tbsp. of sour cream
- 1 tbsp. of fresh celery, finely chopped
- 1 tsp of granulated sugar 2 cups of water
- 1 tbsp. of butter

Method: *(Servings: 6)*

1. Combine the ingredients in a slow cooker and securely close the lid. Set the heat to low and cook for 8 hours.
2. Open the cooker and transfer the soup to a food processor.
3. Blend well to combine and serve.

Calories 194, fat 9.8g, carbs 21.7g, proteins 10g

Gorgonzola Broccoli Soup

Ingredients: *(Time: 2 hours 5 minutes)*

- 10 oz. of Gorgonzola cheese, crumbled
- 1 cup of broccoli, finely chopped
- 1 tbsp. of olive oil
- ½ cup of full-fat milk
- ½ cup of vegetable broth
- 1 tbsp. of parsley, finely chopped
- ½ tsp of salt
- ¼ tsp of black pepper, ground

Method: *(Servings: 4)*

1. Grease the bottom of a slow cooker with olive oil. Add all ingredients and three cups of water. Mix well with a kitchen whisker until fully combined.
2. Cover with a lid and cook for 2 hours on low settings.
3. Remove from the heat and sprinkle with some fresh parsley for extra taste.
4. I like to stir in one tablespoon of Greek yogurt before serving, but it's optional.

Per serving:

Calories 208, Fat 15.8g, Carbs 7.6g, Proteins 11.8g

Spring Spinach Soup

Ingredients: *(Time: 8 hours 20 minutes)*

- 1 lb of lamb shoulder, cut into bite-sized pieces

- 12 oz fresh spinach leaves, torn
- 3 eggs, beaten
- 4 cups of vegetable broth
- 3 tbsp of extra virgin olive oil
- 1 tsp of salt

Method: (Servings: 5).

1. Rinse and drain each spinach leaf. Cut into bite-sized pieces. Place in a slow cooker.
2. Sprinkle the meat generously with salt and transfer to a cooker.
3. Add other ingredients and whisk in three beaten eggs.
4. Close the lid and cook for 8 hours on low.

Per serving

Calories 325, Fat 19g, Carbs 3.4g, Proteins 34.6g

Classic Ragout Soup

Ingredients: (Time: 8 hours 5 minutes)

- 1 lb lamb chops (1 inch thick)
- 1 cup of peas, rinsed
- 4 medium-sized carrots, peeled and finely chopped
- 3 small onions, peeled and finely chopped
- 1 large potato, peeled and finely chopped
- 1 large tomato, peeled and roughly chopped
- 3 tbsp. of extra virgin olive oil
- 1 tbsp. of cayenne pepper
- 1 tsp of salt
- ½ tsp of freshly ground black pepper

Method: (Servings: 6).

1. Cut meat into bite-sized pieces. Make the first layer in your slow cooker.
2. Now add peas, finely chopped carrots, onions, potatoes, and roughly chopped tomato.
3. Add about three tablespoons of olive oil, cayenne pepper, salt, and pepper.
4. Give it a good stir and close the lid. Set for 8 hours on low.

Per serving.

Calories 307, fat 13g, carbs 23.3g, proteins 24.9g

Tomato Soup

Ingredients: (Time: 5 hours 10 minutes)

- 2 lbs of medium-sized tomatoes, diced
- 1 cup of white beans, pre-cooked
- 1 small onion, diced
- 2 garlic cloves, crushed
- 1 cup of heavy cream
- 1 cup of vegetable broth
- 2 tbsp. of fresh parsley, finely chopped
- ¼ tsp of black pepper, ground
- 2 tbsp. of extra virgin olive oil
- 1 tsp of sugar ½ tsp of salt

Method: (Servings: 5).

1. Grease the bottom of your cooker with olive oil. Set the heat to high and heat up.
2. Add chopped onion and garlic. Briefly stir-fry, for 2 minutes.
3. Now add tomatoes, white beans, vegetable broth, two cups of water, parsley, salt, pepper, and some sugar to balance the bitterness.
4. Reduce the heat to low and cook for 5 hours on low, or 3 hours on high.
5. Top with one tablespoon of sour cream and chopped parsley before serving.

Greek Lemon Chicken Soup

Ingredients: *(Time: 4 hours 10 minutes)*

- 2 boneless, skinless chicken breasts
- 4 cups chicken broth
- 1 lemon, juiced
- 1 cup orzo pasta
- ¼ cup fresh dill, chopped

Method: *(Servings: 4).*

1. Place chicken breasts, chicken broth, lemon juice, orzo pasta, and dill in a slow cooker.
2. Cook on low heat for 4 hours or until chicken is cooked through.
3. Shred the chicken using two forks.
4. Serve it hot and enjoy.

Per serving

Calories: 340, fat: 6g, carbs: 35g, protein: 34g

Mediterranean White Bean Soup

Ingredients: *(Time: 6 hours 20 minutes)*

- 2 cans white beans, drained and washed
- 1 onion, diced
- 2 carrots, diced
- 2 celery stalks, diced

- 4 cups veggie soup

Method: *(Servings: 6).*

1. In a slow cooker, mix white beans, onion, carrots, celery, and veggie broth.
2. Cook on low heat for 6 hours or until veggies are soft.
3. Use an immersion mixer to blend some of the soup into a smooth paste while keeping some chunks.
4. Serve it hot and enjoy.

Per serving.

Calories: 220, fat: 1g, carbs: 42g, protein: 13g

Roasted Red Pepper and Tomato Soup

Ingredients: *(Time: 4 hours 10 minutes)*

- 2 roasted red peppers, diced
- 4 tomatoes, diced
- 1 onion, diced
- 3 cloves garlic, minced
- 4 cups veggie soup

Method: *(Servings: 4).*

1. In a slow cooker, mix roasted red peppers, tomatoes, onion, garlic, and veggie broth.
2. Cook on low heat for 4 hours or until veggies are soft.
3. Use an immersion mixer to puree the soup until smooth.
4. Serve it hot and enjoy.

Per serving.

Calories: 140, fat: 1g, carbs: 30g, protein: 5g

Tuscan White Bean Stew

Ingredients: *(Time: 4 hours 10 minutes)*

- 2 cans (15 oz. each) cannellini beans, cleaned and drained
- 1 can (14.5 oz.) diced tomatoes, undrained
- 1 onion, chopped
- 2 cloves garlic, minced
- 1 teaspoon dried rosemary

Method: *(Servings: 4).*

1. In a slow cooker, mix the cannellini beans, diced tomatoes, chopped onion, minced garlic, and dried rosemary.
2. Stir well to mix all the ingredients.
3. Cover and cook on low for 4 hours or until the flavours mix together. 4
4. Serve the stew hot with buttered bread.

Per serving.

Calories: 212, fat: 2g carbs: 40g, protein: 10g

Fish Stew

Ingredients: *(Time: 3-4 hours 10 minutes)*

- 1-pound fresh fish fillets of your choice, cut into 2-inch pieces
- 3 cups low-sodium vegetable broth or low-sodium chicken broth
- 1 (15-ounce) can no-salt-added diced tomatoes
- 1 bell pepper, any color, seeded and diced
- 1 small onion, diced 1 garlic clove, minced
- 1 teaspoon ground coriander
- 1 teaspoon sea salt

- 1 teaspoon paprika
- ½ teaspoon ground turmeric
- ½ teaspoon freshly ground black pepper
- ¼ cup fresh cilantro

Method: *(Servings: 6).*

1. In a slow cooker, combine the fish, vegetable broth, tomatoes, bell pepper, onion, garlic, coriander, salt, paprika, turmeric, and black pepper. Stir to mix well.
2. Cover the cooker and cook for 3 to 5 hours on Low heat.
3. Garnish with the fresh cilantro for serving.
4. Serve this stew over cooked rice (either white or brown) or even riced cauliflower for a light meal.

Per serving:

Calories: 115; fat: 1g; Carbs: 8g; Protein: 18g

Chickpea and Garlic Stew

Ingredients: *(Time: 6-8 hours 10 minutes)*

- 2 cups dried chickpeas, rinsed
- 4 cups low-sodium vegetable broth or low-sodium chicken broth
- 1 tablespoon extra-virgin olive oil
- 1 small onion, diced
- 1 green bell pepper, seeded and chopped
- 2 garlic cloves, minced
- 1 tablespoon drained capers
- 1 teaspoon ground cumin
- 1 teaspoon ground turmeric
- ½ teaspoon ground coriander
- ½ teaspoon sea salt

- ¼ teaspoon freshly ground black pepper

Method: *(Servings: 6).*

1. In a slow cooker, combine the chickpeas, vegetable broth, olive oil, onion, bell pepper, garlic, capers, cumin, turmeric, coriander, salt, and black pepper. Stir to mix well.
2. Cover the cooker and cook for 6 to 8 hours on Low heat.

Per serving:

Calories: 286; fat: 6g; carbs: 45g; protein: 14g

Rosemary-Thyme Stew

Ingredients: *(Time: 8-9 hours 40 minutes)*

- 1 teaspoon canola oil
- 1 large onion, peeled and diced
- 1 tablespoon all-purpose flour
- 1 large carrot, peeled and diced
- 2 stalks celery, diced
- 2 cloves garlic, minced
- 1 cup diced Yukon Gold potatoes
- 3½ tablespoons minced fresh thyme
- 3 tablespoons minced fresh rosemary
- 1 pound boneless, skinless chicken breast, cut into 1" cubes
- ¼ teaspoon kosher salt
- ½ teaspoon freshly ground black pepper
- 1 ½ cups water
- ½ cup frozen or fresh corn kernels

Method: *(Servings: 4).*

1. Heat the oil in a large skillet over medium heat.
2. Sauté the onion, flour, carrots, celery, garlic, potatoes, thyme, rosemary, and chicken until the chicken is white on all sides, about 10 minutes.
3. Using a slotted spoon, transfer to a 4- to 5-quart slow cooker. Stir in salt, pepper, and water.
4. Cook for 8 –9 hours on low. Add the corn.
5. Cover and cook an additional 30 minutes on high. Stir before serving.

Per serving:

Calories: 221, Fat: 4g, Carbs: 18g, Protein: 26g

Beans & Grain

Falafel

Ingredients: (Time: 6-8 hours 10 minutes)

- Non-stick cooking spray
- 2 cups canned reduced-sodium chickpeas, rinsed and drained
- 4 garlic cloves, peeled ¼ cup chickpea flour or all-purpose flour
- ¼ cup diced onion
- ¼ cup chopped fresh parsley
- ¼ cup chopped fresh cilantro
- 1 teaspoon sea salt
- 1 teaspoon ground cumin
- ½ teaspoon ground coriander
- ½ teaspoon freshly ground black pepper
- ⅛ teaspoon cayenne pepper

Method: (Servings: 4).

1. Generously coat a slow cooker insert with cooking spray.
2. In a blender or food processor, combine the chickpeas, garlic, flour, onion, parsley, cilantro, salt, cumin, coriander, black pepper, and cayenne pepper.
3. Process until smooth. Form the mixture into 6 to 8 (2-inch) round patties and place them in a single layer in the prepared slow cooker.
4. Cover the cooker and cook for 6 to 8 hours on Low heat.

Per serving:

Calories: 174; fat: 3g; carbs: 30g; protein: 9g

Ginger Soy Green Beans

Ingredients: (Time: 2 hours 10 minutes)

- 1 pound of fresh green beans, trimmed
- 2 tablespoons of soy sauce
- 1 tablespoon of honey
- 2 cloves of garlic, minced
- 1 teaspoon of ginger, minced
- 2 tablespoons of sesame oil
- Salt and black pepper to taste
- Toasted sesame seeds for garnish (optional)

Method: (Servings: 4).

1. Place the trimmed green beans in the crock pot.
2. In a bowl, whisk together the soy sauce, honey, minced garlic, minced ginger, sesame oil, salt, and black pepper.
3. Drizzle the ginger soy mixture over the green beans and toss to coat.
4. Cover and cook on low for 2 hours or until the green beans are tender and the sauce has reduced and coated the beans.
5. Garnish with toasted sesame seeds before serving, if desired.

Per serving:

Calories: 143; fat: 10g; carb: 13g; protein: 3g

Mediterranean Lentil Casserole

Ingredients: (Time: 8-10 hours 15 minutes)

- 1 pound lentils, rinsed well under cold water and picked over to remove debris
- 4 cups low-sodium vegetable broth
- 3 carrots, diced

- 3 cups chopped kale
- 1 small onion, diced
- 2 garlic cloves, minced
- 1 teaspoon sea salt
- 1 teaspoon dried basil
- 1 teaspoon dried oregano
- ½ teaspoon dried parsley
- 1 lemon, thinly sliced

Method: (Servings: 6).

1. In a slow cooker, combine the lentils, vegetable broth, carrots, kale, onion, garlic, salt, basil, oregano, and parsley. Stir to mix well.
2. Cover the cooker and cook for 8 to 10 hours on Low heat, or until the lentils are tender.
3. Garnish with lemon slices for serving.
4. Garnish this lentil casserole with your favorite toppings, such as chopped fresh mint, cilantro, or even a simple yogurt sauce.

Per serving:

Calories: 302; fat: 2g; carbs: 54g; protein: 22g

Vegan Quinoa and Corn Casserole

Ingredients: (Time: 3 hours 20 minutes)

- 1 cup quinoa, rinsed
- 2 cups vegetable broth
- 1 cup corn kernels (fresh or frozen)
- 1 bell pepper, diced
- 1 onion, diced
- 2 cloves garlic, minced

- ½ cup vegan cheese, shredded
- ¼ cup vegan sour cream
- Salt and pepper to taste
- Chopped fresh chives for garnish

Method: (Servings: 4).

1. In the crock pot, combine quinoa, vegetable broth, corn kernels, diced bell pepper, diced onion, minced garlic, vegan cheese, vegan sour cream, salt, and pepper.
2. Stir well, cover, and cook on low for 3 hours.
3. Garnish with chopped fresh chives before serving as a creamy quinoa and corn casserole.

Per serving:

Calories: 285; fat: 9g; carb: 5g; protein: 11g

Black-Eyed Peas with Ham

Ingredients: (Time: 6-8 hours 15 minutes)

For The Ras Al-Hanout

- 1 teaspoon ground cumin
- 1 teaspoon ground ginger
- 1 teaspoon ground turmeric
- 1 teaspoon paprika
- 1 teaspoon garlic powder
- 1 teaspoon red pepper flakes
- ½ teaspoon ground cinnamon
- ½ teaspoon ground coriander
- ½ teaspoon ground nutmeg

- ½ teaspoon ground cloves

- ½ teaspoon sea salt
- ½ teaspoon freshly ground black pepper

For The Stew

- 1 pound dried black-eyed peas, rinsed well under cold water and picked over to remove debris
- 1 large ham hock
- 5 cups low-sodium chicken broth
- 1 small onion, diced
- 1 bell pepper, any color, seeded and diced
- 2 garlic cloves, minced

Method: *(Servings: 6).*

1. In a small bowl, combine the cumin, ginger, turmeric, paprika, garlic powder, red pepper flakes, cinnamon, coriander, nutmeg, cloves, salt, and black pepper. Mix thoroughly.
2. In a slow cooker, combine the black-eyed peas, ham hock, chicken broth, onion, bell pepper, garlic, and the ras al-hanout. Stir to mix well.
3. Cover the cooker and cook for 6 to 8 hours on Low heat.

Per serving:

Calories: 456; fat: 18g; carbs: 58g; protein: 37g

Crock Pot Rice and Bean Bowl Prep

Ingredients: *(Time: 2 hours 15 minutes)*

- 1 small onion, chopped
- 2 tsp. minced garlic
- 2 15 oz. cans black beans, rinsed well and drained
- 1 cup uncooked brown rice

- 2 4 oz. cans diced green chilies
- 1 14 oz. can vegetable broth
- 1/2 tsp. ground cumin
- 1 tsp. Mexican oregano
- 2 tsp. Sazon seasoning (optional, but it adds a lot of flavor)
- 6 pieces Mozzarella string cheese
- 1 cup green onions, sliced (more or less to taste)

Method: (Servings: 4).

1. Spray the inside of a slow cooker with non-stick spray. Chop up the onion.
2. If using canned beans, rinse in a colander placed in the sink (until no more foam appears) and let the beans drain.
3. Put diced onion, minced garlic, black beans, rice, vegetable broth, diced green chilies, ground cumin, Mexican oregano, and Sazon (if using) into the slow cooker.
4. Cook on high for 1 hour 30 minutes. Cut 6 sticks Mozzarella string cheese into slices (or cut 6 oz. cheese into cubes if not using string cheese.)
5. Gently stir the cheese into the rice and bean mixture and cook 20-30 more minutes, or until the rice is done and the cheese is melting.
6. Chop up desired amount of green onions. Turn off heat, stir in the green onions, and serve hot with salsa, diced avocado, and/or sour cream to add at the table.

Per serving:

Calories: 1197; fat: 17g; carb: 202g; protein: 62g

Pork and White Bean Stew

Ingredients: (Time: 6-8 hours 45 minutes)

- 2 pounds' boneless pork shoulder or butt, cut into 1-inch cubes
- 1 (15-ounce) can reduced-sodium white beans, drained and rinsed

- 2 cups low-sodium vegetable broth or low-sodium chicken broth
- 1 (15-ounce) can no-salt-added diced tomatoes
- 1 small onion, diced
- 2 garlic cloves, minced
- 1½ teaspoons dried rosemary
- 1 teaspoon sea salt
- ½ teaspoon freshly ground black pepper
- 4 ounces' fresh spinach, chopped

Method: (Servings: 6)

1. In a slow cooker, combine the pork, beans, vegetable broth, tomatoes, onion, garlic, rosemary, salt, and pepper. Stir to mix well.
2. Cover the cooker and cook for 6 to 8 hours on Low heat.
3. Stir in the spinach, replace the cover on the cooker, and cook for 15 to 30 minutes on Low heat, or until the spinach wilts.

Per serving:

Calories: 370; fat: 19g; carbs: 17g; protein: 32g

Black Bean and Brown Rice Salad

Ingredients: (Time: 2 hours 1 minutes)

- 1 cup brown rice
- 2 cups vegetable broth
- 2 cans (15 oz. each) black beans, drained and rinsed
- 1 bell pepper, diced
- ½ cup red onion, finely chopped
- ¼ cup fresh cilantro, chopped
- Zest and juice of 2 limes
- Salt and pepper to taste

1. In the crock pot, combine brown rice, vegetable broth, black beans, diced bell pepper, finely chopped red onion, chopped fresh cilantro, lime zest, lime juice, salt, and pepper.
2. Stir well, cover, and cook on low for 2 hours or until the rice is cooked.
3. Fluff with a fork before serving this zesty black bean and brown rice salad.

Per serving:

Calories: 550; fat: 2.99g; carb: 108.6g; protein: 24.73g

Za'atar Chickpeas and Chicken

Ingredients: (Time: 4-6 hours 10 minutes)

- 2 pounds bone-in chicken thighs or legs
- 1 (15-ounce) can reduced-sodium chickpeas, drained and rinsed
- ½ cup low-sodium chicken broth
- Juice of 1 lemon
- 1 tablespoon extra-virgin olive oil
- 2 teaspoons white vinegar
- 2 tablespoons za'atar
- 1 garlic clove, minced
- ½ teaspoon sea salt
- ¼ teaspoon freshly ground black pepper

Method: (Servings: 4).

1. In a slow cooker, combine the chicken and chickpeas. Stir to mix well.
2. In a small bowl, whisk together the chicken broth, lemon juice, olive oil, vinegar, za'atar, garlic, salt, and pepper until combined.
3. Pour the mixture over the chicken and chickpeas.
4. Cover the cooker and cook for 4 to 6 hours on Low heat.

Per serving:

Calories: 647; fat: 41g; carbs: 23g; protein: 46g

Sweet Potato Black Bean Chili

Ingredients: *(Time: 4 hours 20 minutes)*

- 2 medium sweet potatoes, peeled and cubed
- 1 medium yellow onion, finely chopped
- 1 poblano pepper, seeds removed, finely chopped
- 4 garlic cloves, minced
- 2 (15-oz.) cans black beans, rinsed and drained
- 1 (15-oz.) can dark red kidney beans, rinsed and drained
- 2 (14.5-oz.) cans fire-roasted diced tomatoes with green chilies
- 1 cup vegetable broth (sub beef or bone broth if not making vegetarian)
- 2 Tbsp. tomato paste
- 2 Tbsp. chili powder
- 1 Tbsp. ground cumin
- 2 tsp. smoked paprika
- 1 tsp. dried oregano
- 2 tsp. kosher salt

Method: *(Servings: 4).*

1. Grease a slow cooker with non-stick cooking spray.
2. Combine all chili ingredients; stir well to combine.
3. Cook on low for 8 hours, or on high for 4 hours, until the sweet potatoes are tender.
4. Serve with your favorite toppings.

Per serving:

Calories: 392; fat: 3.71g; carb: 72.13g; protein: 21.46g

Lentil Bowl

Ingredients: (Time: 6-8 hours 10 minutes)

- 1 cup dried lentils, any color, rinsed
- 3 cups low-sodium vegetable broth
- 1 (15-ounce) can no-salt-added diced tomatoes
- 1 small onion, chopped
- 3 celery stalks, chopped
- 3 carrots, chopped
- 3 garlic cloves, minced
- 2 tablespoons Italian seasoning
- 1 teaspoon sea salt
- ½ teaspoon freshly ground black pepper
- 2 bay leaves
- 1 tablespoon freshly squeezed lemon juice

Method: (Servings: 6).

1. In a slow cooker, combine the lentils, vegetable broth, tomatoes, onion, celery, carrots, garlic, Italian seasoning, salt, pepper, and bay leaves. Stir to mix well.
2. Cover the cooker and cook for 6 to 8 hours on Low heat.
3. Stir in the lemon juice before serving.

Per serving:

Calories: 152; fat: 1g; carbs: 29g; protein: 10g

Fava Beans with Ground Meat

Ingredients: (Time: 6-8 hours 15 minutes)

- 8 ounces' raw ground meat

- 1 pound dried fava beans, rinsed and picked
- 10 cups water or 5 cups water and 5 cups low-sodium vegetable broth
- 1 small onion, diced
- 1 bell pepper, any color, seeded and diced
- 1 teaspoon sea salt
- 1 teaspoon garlic powder
- 1 teaspoon dried parsley 1
- teaspoon dried oregano
- 1 teaspoon paprika
- 1 teaspoon cayenne pepper
- ½ teaspoon freshly ground black pepper
- ½ teaspoon dried thyme

Method: (Servings: 6).

1. In a large skillet over medium-high heat, cook the ground meat for 3 to 5 minutes, stirring and breaking it up with a spoon, until it has browned and is no longer pink.
2. Drain any grease and put the meat in a slow cooker.
3. Add the fava beans, water, onion, bell pepper, salt, garlic powder, parsley, oregano, paprika, cayenne pepper, black pepper, and thyme to the meat. Stir to mix well.
4. Cover the cooker and cook for 6 to 8 hours on Low heat, or until the beans are tender.

Per serving:

Calories: 308; fat: 4g; carbs: 43g; protein: 26g

Barley and Vegetable Casserole

Ingredients: (Time: 8 hours 10 minutes)

- 1 cup raw barley (not the quick-cooking type)

- 3 cups low-sodium vegetable broth
- 3 garlic cloves, minced
- 2 bell peppers, any color, seeded and chopped
- 1 small onion, chopped 2 ounces mushrooms, sliced
- 1 teaspoon extra-virgin olive oil
- 2 tablespoons Italian seasoning
- 1 teaspoon sea salt
- ¼ teaspoon freshly ground black pepper

Method: (Servings: 6).

1. In a slow cooker, combine the barley, vegetable broth, garlic, bell peppers, onion, mushrooms, olive oil, Italian seasoning, salt, and black pepper. Stir to mix well.
2. Cover the cooker and cook for 6 to 8 hours on Low heat.

Per serving:

Calories: 147; fat: 2g; carbs: 30g; protein: 5g

Bulgur-Stuffed Portobello Mushrooms

Ingredients: (Time: 8 hours 15 minutes)

1. 1½ cups cooked bulgur
2. 2 zucchini, diced
3. ¼ cup diced onion
4. 2 garlic cloves, minced
5. 1 teaspoon sea salt
6. 1 teaspoon ground cumin
7. ½ teaspoon freshly ground black pepper
8. 1 (28-ounce) can no-salt-added crushed tomatoes
9. 4 portobello mushrooms, stemmed, gills removed, wiped clean

Method: (Servings: 4).

1. In a medium bowl, stir together the bulgur, zucchini, onion, garlic, salt, cumin, and pepper.
2. Put the tomatoes in a slow cooker.
3. Evenly stuff each portobello mushroom cap with the bulgur mixture. Place the mushrooms on top of the tomatoes in a single layer.
4. Cover the cooker and cook for 6 to 8 hours on Low heat.

per serving:

Calories: 144; fat: 1g; carbs: 32g; Protein: 7g

Herbed Polenta

Ingredients: *(Time: 4-5 hours 40 minutes)*

1. 1 cup stone-ground polenta
2. 4 cups low-sodium vegetable stock or low-sodium chicken stock
3. 1 tablespoon extra-virgin olive oil
4. 1 small onion, minced
5. 2 garlic cloves, minced
6. 1 teaspoon sea salt
7. 1 teaspoon dried parsley
8. 1 teaspoon dried oregano
9. 1 teaspoon dried thyme
10. ½ teaspoon freshly ground black pepper
11. ½ cup grated Parmesan cheese

Method: *(Servings: 4).*

1. In a slow cooker, combine the polenta, vegetable stock, olive oil, onion, garlic, salt, parsley, oregano, thyme, and pepper. Stir to mix well.
2. Cover the cooker and cook for 3 to 5 hours on Low heat.
3. Stir in the Parmesan cheese for serving.

Mediterranean Quinoa and Vegetable Pilaf

Ingredients: (Time: 4 hours 20 minutes)

- 1 cup quinoa, rinsed
- 2 cups vegetable broth
- 1 cup cherry tomatoes, halved
- 1 cup bell peppers (mixed colors), diced
- 1 cup artichoke hearts, quartered
- ½ cup kalamata olives, sliced
- 3 cloves garlic, minced
- 1 teaspoon dried basil
- 1 teaspoon dried oregano
- Salt and pepper to taste
- 2 tablespoons olive oil

Method: (Servings: 6-8).

1. Combine quinoa, vegetable broth, cherry tomatoes, bell peppers, artichoke hearts, olives, minced garlic, dried basil, and dried oregano in the Crock Pot.
2. Season with salt and pepper. Drizzle olive oil over the ingredients.
3. Stir gently to mix everything together.
4. Cover and cook on low for 4 hours or until quinoa is tender.
5. Fluff the quinoa with a fork before serving. Adjust seasoning if needed.

Per serving:

Calories: 157; fat: 6.44; carb: 21.45; protein: 4.65

Wild Rice and Mushroom Pilaf

Ingredients: (Time: 4 hours 20 minutes)

- 1 cup wild rice, uncooked
- 2 cups vegetable broth
- 1 cup cremini mushrooms, sliced
- 1 cup leeks, thinly sliced
- 3 cloves garlic, minced
- ½ cup sun-dried tomatoes, chopped
- 1 teaspoon dried thyme
- 1 teaspoon dried rosemary
- Salt and pepper to taste
- 2 tablespoons olive oil
- ¼ cup fresh parsley, chopped (for garnish)

Method: (Servings: 4-6).

1. In the Crock Pot, combine wild rice, vegetable broth, sliced cremini mushrooms, sliced leeks, minced garlic, chopped sun-dried tomatoes, dried thyme, and dried rosemary.
2. Season with salt and pepper. Drizzle olive oil over the ingredients. Stir well.
3. Cover and cook on low for 4 hours or until the wild rice is tender.
4. Before serving, garnish with fresh parsley. Adjust seasoning if necessary.

Per serving:

Calories: 199; fat: 6.03g; carb: 32.44g; protein: 6.18g

Black Bean and Quinoa Stuffed Bell Peppers

Ingredients: (Time: 4 hours 20 minutes)

- 4 bell peppers, tops removed and seeds removed

- 1 cup quinoa, rinsed
- 2 cups vegetable broth
- 2 cans (15 oz. each) black beans, drained and rinsed
- 1 can (14 oz.) diced tomatoes
- 1 teaspoon chili powder
- Salt and pepper to taste
- Sliced avocado for garnish

Method: (Servings: 4).

1. Stuff each bell pepper with quinoa, black beans, diced tomatoes, chili powder, salt, and pepper.
2. Place the stuffed peppers in the crock pot.
3. Cover and cook on low for 4 hours or until the peppers are tender.
4. Garnish with sliced avocado before serving.

Per serving:

Calories: 555; fat: 11.42g; carb: 90.78g; protein: 27.44g

Chickpea Stew

Ingredients: (Time: 3 hours 10 minutes)

- 1 tablespoon olive oil
- 1 small white onion diced
- 2 garlic cloves minced
- 1 tablespoon minced fresh ginger
- 1 teaspoon cumin
- 1 teaspoon paprika
- ¼ teaspoon coriander
- ¼ teaspoon cinnamon
- ¼ teaspoon ginger

- 1 teaspoon kosher salt
- ½ teaspoon black pepper
- 1-14.5 ounce can chickpeas drained and rinsed
- 1-14.5 ounce can diced fire-roasted tomatoes
- 1 medium sweet potato diced
- 2 carrots trimmed and diced
- 1 red pepper diced
- 1 cup green lentils
- 2 tablespoons harissa paste
- 4 cups low sodium vegetable broth
- Chopped parsley for serving

Method: (Servings: 6).

1. In a skillet or stove-top safe slow cooker pot, heat the olive oil over medium heat. Sauté the onions until they are soft and translucent, about 5-7 minutes.
2. Add the minced garlic, minced fresh ginger, dried spices (cumin, paprika, coriander, cinnamon & ginger), salt and pepper. Cook until fragrant, about 1 minute.
3. Transfer the onions to the slow cooker. Add the chickpeas, tomatoes, sweet potatoes, carrots, red peppers, lentils, harissa and vegetable broth.
4. Cook on high for 3-4 hours or on low for 6-7 hours until the vegetables and lentils are tender. 4.
5. Divide into bowls and garnish with chopped parsley before serving.

Per serving:

Calories: 183; fat: 4.98g; carb: 31.11g; protein: 7.18g

Barley and Mushroom Risotto

Ingredients: (Time: 3 hours 10 minutes)

- 2 tablespoons extra-virgin olive oil
- 1 large onion, finely chopped
- Kosher salt and freshly ground black pepper
- 1 pound cremini mushrooms, sliced
- 1 ½ cups pearl barley
- 4 sprigs fresh thyme
- 8 ounces' carrots, finely chopped
- 3 cups lower-sodium vegetable broth
- 1-ounce Parmesan, grated (2/3 cup)
- 1 tablespoon sherry vinegar
- ¼ cup chopped fresh flat-leaf parsley

Method: (Servings: 4).

1. Heat the olive oil in a large skillet over medium-high heat. Add the onions and 1/8 teaspoon each salt and pepper and cook, stirring occasionally, until lightly browned, about 5 minutes.
2. Add the mushrooms and cook, stirring occasionally, until browned, about 2 minutes. Stir in the barley and thyme and cook, stirring, until the barley is just golden, about 2 minutes.
3. Transfer to a slow cooker and add the carrots, broth, 1 1/2 cups water and 1/4 teaspoon salt. Cover and cook on high until the liquid is absorbed and the carrots and barley are tender, about 3 hours.
4. Discard the thyme and stir in the Parmesan, vinegar, 1/2 teaspoon salt and 1/4 teaspoon pepper. Thin out the risotto with warm water for desired consistency as needed.
5. Top with parsley and season to taste with salt and pepper.

Per serving:

Calories: 706; fat: 6.33g; carb: 156.2g; protein: 23.19g

Vegetables

Eggplant "Lasagna"

Ingredients: (Time: 6-8 hours 10 minutes)

- 2 medium globe eggplants, peeled and thinly sliced
- 1 teaspoon sea salt, plus more for the eggplant
- 2 cups cottage cheese
- ½ cup ricotta
- 1 large egg
- ½ teaspoon freshly ground black pepper
- 1 (28-ounce) can no-salt-added diced tomatoes
- 1 small onion, diced
- 1 bell pepper, any color, seeded and diced
- 4 ounces' mushrooms, sliced

Method: (Servings: 4).

1. Lay the eggplant slices on paper towels in a single layer and lightly sprinkle them with salt. Let them sit for 10 to 30 minutes to draw out excess moisture.
2. In a medium bowl, stir together the cottage cheese, ricotta, egg, the remaining 1 teaspoon of salt, and black pepper.
3. Cover the bottom of a slow cooker with one-quarter of the tomatoes.
4. Blot the eggplant slices with a paper towel to remove the excess liquid and salt.
5. Layer one-quarter each of the eggplant, onion, bell pepper, mushrooms, and cottage cheese mixture. Repeat the layers in the same sequence until all of the ingredients are used.
6. Cover the cooker and cook for 6 to 8 hours on Low heat. Let cool slightly before slicing and serving.

Per serving:

Calories: 204; fat: 7g; carbs: 23g; protein: 15g

Egg Casserole with Tomato, Spinach, and Feta

Ingredients: (Time: 6-8 hours 10 minutes)

- 12 large eggs
- ¼ cup milk of your choice
- 1 cup fresh spinach, chopped
- ¼ cup feta cheese, crumbled
- ½ teaspoon sea salt
- ¼ teaspoon freshly ground black pepper
- Non-stick cooking spray
- 2 Roma tomatoes, sliced

Method: (Servings: 6).

Per serving:

1. In a medium bowl, whisk together the eggs, milk, spinach, feta cheese, salt, and pepper until combined.
2. Generously coat a slow-cooker insert with cooking spray.
3. Pour the egg mixture into the slow cooker. Top with the tomato slices.
4. Cover the cooker and cook for 6 to 8 hours on Low heat.

Per serving:

Calories: 178; fat: 11g; Carbs: 4g; Protein: 14g

Vegetable Terrine

Ingredients: (Time: 5-7 hours 30 minutes)

- 1 small eggplant, thinly sliced lengthwise
- 2 green bell peppers, halved, seeded, and sliced

- 2 red bell peppers, halved, seeded, and sliced
- 1 portobello mushroom, cut into ¼-inch-thick slices
- 1 zucchini, thinly sliced lengthwise
- 1 large red onion, cut into ¼-inch-thick rounds
- 2 yellow squash, thinly sliced lengthwise
- 4 large tomatoes, sliced
- 1 teaspoon sea salt
- ¼ teaspoon freshly ground black pepper
- Non-stick cooking spray
- 1 cup grated Parmesan cheese
- 2 tablespoons extra-virgin olive oil
- 1 tablespoon red wine vinegar
- 2 teaspoons freshly squeezed lemon juice
- 1 teaspoon dried basil 1 garlic clove, minced

Method: (Servings: 6).

Per serving:

1. Season the eggplant, green and red bell peppers, mushroom, zucchini, onion, squash, and tomatoes with salt and black pepper, but keep all the vegetables separate.
2. Generously coat a slow-cooker insert with cooking spray, or line the bottom and sides with parchment paper or aluminum foil.
3. Starting with half of the eggplant, line the bottom of the prepared slow cooker with overlapping slices. Sprinkle with 2 tablespoons of Parmesan cheese.
4. Add a second layer using half of the green and red bell peppers. Sprinkle with 2 more tablespoons of Parmesan cheese.
5. Add a third layer using half of the mushroom slices. Sprinkle with 2 more tablespoons of Parmesan cheese.
6. Add a fourth layer using half of the zucchini slices. Sprinkle with 2 more tablespoons of Parmesan cheese. Add a fifth layer using half of the red onion slices. Sprinkle with another 2 tablespoons of Parmesan cheese.

7. Add a sixth layer using half of the yellow squash slices. Sprinkle with 2 more tablespoons of Parmesan cheese. Add a final seventh layer with half of the tomato slices. Sprinkle with 2 more tablespoons of Parmesan cheese. 1
8. Repeat the layering with the remaining vegetables and Parmesan cheese in the same order until all of the vegetables have been used.
9. In a small bowl, whisk together the olive oil, vinegar, lemon juice, basil, and garlic until combined. Pour the mixture over the vegetables. Top with any remaining Parmesan cheese.
10. Cover the cooker and cook for 5 to 7 hours on Low heat. 13.Let cool to room temperature before slicing and serving

Per serving:

Calories: 217; fat: 11g; carbs: 24g; protein: 12g

Baba Ghanoush

Ingredients: (Time: 2-4 hours 15 minutes)

- 1 large eggplant (2 to 4 pounds), peeled and diced
- ¼ cup freshly squeezed lemon juice
- 2 garlic cloves, minced
- 2 tablespoons tahini
- 1 teaspoon extra-virgin olive oil, plus more as needed
- ¼ teaspoon sea salt, plus more as needed
- ⅛ teaspoon freshly ground black pepper, plus more as needed
- 2 tablespoons chopped fresh parsley

Method: (Servings: 6).

1. In a slow cooker, combine the eggplant, lemon juice, garlic, tahini, olive oil, salt, and pepper. Stir to mix well.
2. Cover the cooker and cook for 2 to 4 hours on Low heat.

3. Using a spoon or potato masher, mash the mixture.
4. If you prefer a smoother texture, transfer it to a food processor and blend to your desired consistency. Taste and season with olive oil, salt, and pepper as needed.
5. Garnish with fresh parsley for serving.

Per serving:

Calories: 81; fat: 4g; carbs: 12g; Protein: 3g

Steamed Vegetables

Ingredients: (Time: 5-7 hours 10 minutes)

- 2 pounds' fresh vegetables of your choice, sliced
- 1 teaspoon dried thyme
- 1 teaspoon dried rosemary
- 1 teaspoon sea salt
- ¼ teaspoon freshly ground black pepper
- 2 tablespoons extra-virgin olive oil

Method: (Servings: 6).

1. Put the vegetables in a slow cooker and season them with thyme, rosemary, salt, and pepper.
2. Drizzle the olive oil on top.
3. Cover the cooker and cook for 5 to 7 hours on Low heat, or until the vegetables are tender.

Per serving:

Calories: 85; fat: 5g; carbs: 11g; protein: 1g

Stuffed Artichokes

Ingredients: *(Time: 5-7 hours 20 minutes)*

- 4 to 6 fresh large artichokes
- ½ cup bread crumbs
- ½ cup grated Parmesan cheese or Romano cheese
- 4 garlic cloves, minced
- ½ teaspoon sea salt
- ½ teaspoon freshly ground black pepper
- ¼ cup water
- 2 tablespoons extra-virgin olive oil
- 2 tablespoons chopped fresh parsley for garnish (optional)

Method: *(Servings: 4-6).*

1. To trim and prepare the artichokes, cut off the bottom along with 1 inch from the top of each artichoke.
2. Pull off and discard the lowest leaves nearest the stem end. Trim off any pointy tips of artichoke leaves that are poking out. Set aside.
3. In a small bowl, stir together the bread crumbs, Parmesan cheese, garlic, salt, and pepper.
4. Spread apart the artichoke leaves and stuff the bread-crumb mixture into the spaces, down to the base.
5. Pour the water into a slow cooker.
6. Place the artichokes in the slow cooker in a single layer. Drizzle the olive oil over the artichokes.
7. Cover the cooker and cook for 5 to 7 hours on Low heat, or until the artichokes are tender. Garnish with fresh parsley if desired.

Per serving:

Calories: 224; fat: 12g; carbs: 23g; protein: 12g

Zucchini Parmesan Casserole

Ingredients: *(Time: 5-7 hours 10 minutes)*

- 1 (15-ounce) can no-salt-added diced tomatoes
- 6 zucchini, cut into ¼-inch-thick rounds
- 2 tablespoons unsalted butter, melted
- 1 small onion, chopped
- 2 garlic cloves, minced
- 1 teaspoon garlic powder
- 1 teaspoon dried oregano
- 1 teaspoon sea salt
- ½ teaspoon dried basil
- ¼ teaspoon freshly ground black pepper
- 1 cup grated Parmesan cheese

Method: *(Servings: 4).*

1. Put the tomatoes in a slow cooker.
2. In a large bowl, stir together the zucchini, melted butter, onion, garlic, garlic powder, oregano, salt, basil, and pepper.
3. Pour the zucchini mixture over the tomatoes.
4. Spread the Parmesan cheese on top of the zucchini mixture.
5. Cover the cooker and cook for 5 to 7 hours on Low heat.

Per serving:

Calories: 247; fat: 14g; carbs: 19g; protein: 16g

Mediterranean Ratatouille

Ingredients: *(Time: 5-7 hours 10 minutes)*

- 1 (15-ounce) can no-salt-added diced tomatoes

- 2 zucchini, chopped
- 1 small eggplant, peeled and cubed
- 1 green or red bell pepper, seeded and chopped
- 1 small onion, chopped
- 3 garlic cloves, minced
- 1 tablespoon extra-virgin olive oil
- 1 tablespoon red wine vinegar
- 1 teaspoon sea salt
- 1 teaspoon dried thyme
- 1 teaspoon dried oregano
- 1 teaspoon smoked paprika
- ½ teaspoon freshly ground black pepper
- ¼ cup chopped fresh basil

Method: (Servings: 6).

1. In a slow cooker, combine the tomatoes, zucchini, eggplant, bell pepper, onion, garlic, olive oil, vinegar, salt, thyme, oregano, paprika, and black pepper. Stir to mix well.
2. Cover the cooker and cook for 5 to 7 hours on Low heat.

Per serving:

Calories: 80; fat: 3g; carbs: 14g; protein: 3g

Potato Vegetable Hash

Ingredients: (Time: 5-7 hours 20 minutes)

- 1½ pounds red potatoes, diced
- 8 ounces' green beans, trimmed and cut into ½-inch pieces
- 4 ounces' mushrooms, chopped
- 1 large tomato, chopped

- 1 large zucchini, diced
- 1 small onion, diced
- 1 red bell pepper, seeded and chopped
- ⅓ cup low-sodium vegetable broth
- 1 teaspoon sea salt
- ½ teaspoon garlic powder
- ½ teaspoon freshly ground black pepper
- ¼ teaspoon red pepper flakes
- ¼ cup shredded cheese of your choice (optional)

Method: (Servings: 4).

1. In a slow cooker, combine the potatoes, green beans, mushrooms, tomato, zucchini, onion, bell pepper, vegetable broth, salt, garlic powder, black pepper, and red pepper flakes. Stir to mix well.
2. Cover the cooker and cook for 5 to 7 hours on Low heat.
3. Garnish with cheese for serving (if using).

Per serving:

Calories: 183; fat: 1g; carbs: 41g; protein: 7g

Greek Fasolakia (Green Beans)

Ingredients: (Time: 6-8 hours 10 minutes)

- 2 pounds green beans, trimmed
- 1 (15-ounce) can no-salt-added diced tomatoes, with juice
- 1 large onion, chopped
- 4 garlic cloves, chopped
- Juice of 1 lemon
- 1 teaspoon dried dill
- 1 teaspoon ground cumin

- 1 teaspoon dried oregano
- 1 teaspoon sea salt
- ½ teaspoon freshly ground black pepper
- ¼ cup feta cheese, crumbled

Method: *(Servings: 6).*

1. In a slow cooker, combine the green beans, tomatoes and their juice, onion, garlic, lemon juice, dill, cumin, oregano, salt, and pepper. Stir to mix well.
2. Cover the cooker and cook for 6 to 8 hours on Low heat.
3. Top with feta cheese for serving.

Per serving:

Calories: 94; fat: 2g; carbs: 18g; protein: 5g

Barbunya Pilaki

Ingredients: *(Time: 8-10 hours 20 minutes)*

- 2 cups of cranberry beans
- 2 medium-sized onions, peeled and finely chopped
- 3 large carrots, cleaned and chopped
- 3 large tomatoes, peeled and finely chopped
- 3 tbsp. of extra virgin olive oil
- 2 tsp of granulated sugar
- A handful of fresh parsley
- 2 cups of water

Method: *(Servings: 6).*

1. Soak the beans overnight. Rinse and set aside.
2. Grease the bottom of your slow cooker with olive oil.
3. Add other ingredients and pour two cups of water.

4. Securely lock the lid and set the heat to low. Cook for 8-10 hours.

Per serving:

Calories 329, fat 8g, carbs 50.9g, proteins 16.5g

Balsamic Brussels Sprouts

Ingredients: (Time: 4 hours 20 minutes)

- 2 tablespoons brown sugar
- ½ cup balsamic vinegar
- 2 lb. Brussels sprouts, trimmed and sliced in half
- 2 tablespoons olive oil
- 2 tablespoons butter, sliced into cubes
- Salt and pepper to taste
- ¼ cup Parmesan cheese, grated

Method: (Servings: 6).

1. In a saucepan over medium heat, add the brown sugar and vinegar. Mix and bring to a boil.
2. Reduce heat and simmer for 8 minutes. Let cool and set aside.
3. Toss the Brussels sprouts in olive oil and butter.
4. Season with salt and pepper. Cover the pot. Cook low for 4 hours.
5. Drizzle the balsamic vinegar on top of the Brussels sprouts.
6. Sprinkle the Parmesan cheese on top.

Per serving:

Calories 193, fat 10 g, carbs 21.9 g, protein 6.9 g

Mediterranean Zucchini & Eggplant

Ingredients: (Time: 3 hours 15 minutes)

- 1 tablespoon olive oil
- 1 onion, diced
- 4 cloves garlic, minced
- 1 red bell pepper, chopped
- 4 tomatoes, diced
- 1 zucchini, chopped
- 1 lb. eggplant, sliced into cubes
- Salt and pepper to taste
- 2 teaspoons dried basil
- 4 oz. feta cheese

Method: (Servings: 4).

1. Coat your slow cooker with olive oil.
2. Combine all the ingredients except cheese in the pot.
3. Place the lid and cook on high for 3 hours.
4. Sprinkle feta cheese on top and serve.

Per serving:

Calories 34, fat 12 g, carbs 51 g, protein 13 g

Roasted Baby Carrots

Ingredients: (Time: 6 hours 15 minutes)

- 2 lb. baby carrots
- ¼ cup apricot preserve
- 6 tablespoons butter
- 2 tablespoons honey

- 1 tablespoon sugar
- 1 teaspoon balsamic vinegar
- 1 teaspoon garlic powder
- Salt and pepper to taste
- ¼ teaspoon dried thyme
- ¼ teaspoon ground mustard

Method: (Servings: 6).

1. Combine all the ingredients in the slow cooker.
2. Mix well. Cover the pot. Cook on low for 6 hours.

Per serving:

Calories 218, Fat 11.8g, Carbs 29.3g, Protein 1.3g

Artichokes with Garlic & Cream Sauce

Ingredients: (Time: 8 hours 15 minutes)

- Cooking spray
- 30 oz. canned diced tomatoes
- 6 cloves garlic, crushed and minced
- 28 oz. canned artichoke hearts, rinsed, drained and sliced into quarters
- ½ cup whipping cream
- 1 teaspoon dried basil
- ½ teaspoon dried oregano
- Feta cheese

Method: (Servings: 6).

1. Spray the slow cooker with oil.
2. Add the tomatoes with juice, garlic and artichoke hearts.
3. Season with the basil and oregano. Mix well.

4. Cover the pot and cook on low for 8 hours.
5. Stir in the cream. Let sit for 5 minutes. Top with the crumbled cheese.

Per serving:

Calories 403, fat 5 g, carbs 38 g, protein 13 g

Mediterranean Kale & White Kidney Beans

Ingredients: *(Time: 3 hours 40 minutes)*

- 1 onion, chopped
- 4 cloves garlic, crushed
- ¼ cup celery, chopped
- 2 carrots, sliced
- 1 cup farro, rinsed and drained
- 14 oz. canned roasted tomatoes
- 4 cups low-sodium vegetable broth
- ½ teaspoon red pepper, crushed
- Salt to taste
- 3 tablespoons freshly squeezed lemon juice
- 15 oz. white kidney beans, rinsed and drained
- 4 cup kale
- ½ cup feta cheese, crumbled
- Fresh parsley, chopped

Method: *(Servings: 6).*

1. Put the onion, garlic, celery, carrots, farro, tomatoes, broth, red pepper and salt in your slow cooker. Seal the pot.
2. Cook on high for 2 hours. Stir in the lemon juice, beans and kale.
3. Cover and cook for 1 more hours.
4. Sprinkle the cheese and parsley before serving.

Creamed Corn

Ingredients: (Time: 4 hours 10 minutes)

- 16 oz. frozen corn kernels
- 8 oz. cream cheese
- ½ cup butter
- ½ cup milk
- 1 tablespoon white sugar
- Salt and pepper to taste

Method: (Servings: 12).

1. Put all the ingredients in the slow cooker. Stir well.
2. Cook on high for 4 hours.

Per serving:

Calories 192, fat 15 g, carbs13.7 g, protein 3.4 g

Spicy Beans & Veggies

Ingredients: (Time: 8 hours 20 minutes)

- 15 oz. canned northern beans, rinsed and drained
- 15 oz. canned red beans, rinsed and drained
- 5 teaspoons garlic, minced
- 1 onion, chopped
- 1 cup, sliced thinly
- ½ cup celery, sliced thinly

- 2 cups green beans, trimmed and sliced
- 2 red chili peppers, chopped
- 2 bay leaves
- Salt and pepper to taste

Method: *(Servings: 6).*

1. Combine all the ingredients in the slow cooker. Set it to low.
2. Seal and cook for 8 hours.
3. Discard the bay leaves before serving.

Per serving:

Calories 264 fat 0.9g, carbs 49g, protein 17.2g

Eggplant Salad

Ingredients: *(Time: 8 hours 10 minutes)*

- 1 onion, sliced

- 1 green bell pepper, sliced
- 1 red bell pepper, sliced
- 24 oz. canned tomatoes
- 1 eggplant, sliced
- 2 teaspoons cumin
- 1 tablespoon smoked paprika
- 1 tablespoon lemon juice
- Salt and pepper to taste

Method: *(Servings: 4).*

1. Add all the ingredients to the slow cooker.
2. Mix well. Set it to low.
3. Cover the pot. Cook for 8 hours.

Cinnamon Sugar Butternut Squash

Ingredients: (Time: 3 hours 20 minutes)

- 3-4-pound butternut squash
- ½ cup butter 1 stick
- ¾ cup packed brown sugar
- 1 tsp. ground cinnamon
- ¼ tsp. ground nutmeg
- 1 pinch ground cloves
- 1 dash salt

Method: (Servings: 8).

1. Peel the squash with a potato peeler. Cut in half length wise, then cut into 1-inch cubes.
2. Place the squash into the slow cooker. Cut the butter into slices. Place the butter pats all over the cut squash.
3. In a small bowl mix together the brown sugar, cinnamon, nutmeg, cloves, and salt. Sprinkle this mixture over the squash and butter.
4. Cover and cook on high for 3 hours without opening the lid during the cooking time.
5. Serve and enjoy.

Per serving:

Calories: 243; fat: 8 g; carb: 4 g; protein: 3 g

Rice & Pasta

Mediterranean Pasta Puttanesca

Ingredients: *(Time: 4 hours 15 minutes)*

- 1 pound penne pasta, cooked al dente
- 1 can (14 oz) diced tomatoes
- ½ cup Kalamata olives, sliced
- ¼ cup capers
- 3 cloves garlic, minced
- 1 teaspoon red pepper flakes
- 2 tablespoons olive oil
- ¼ cup fresh basil, chopped
- Salt and pepper to taste
- Grated Parmesan cheese for serving

Method: *(Servings: 4-6).*

1. In the Crock Pot, combine cooked penne pasta, diced tomatoes, sliced Kalamata olives, capers, minced garlic, red pepper flakes, olive oil, and chopped fresh basil.
2. Season with salt and pepper. Stir well.
3. Cover and cook on low for 4 hours, allowing flavors to meld.
4. Before serving, sprinkle with grated Parmesan cheese. Adjust seasoning if necessary.

Per serving:

Calories: 198; fat: 7.71; carb: 30.29; protein: 3.75

Crock Pot Pasta e Fagioli

Ingredients: *(Time: 5 hours 15 minutes)*

- 1 cup ditalini pasta, uncooked
- 2 cans (15 oz. each) cannellini beans, drained and rinsed
- 1 can (14 oz.) diced tomatoes
- 1 cup celery, diced
- 1 cup carrots, diced
- 1 large onion, finely chopped
- 3 cloves garlic, minced
- 4 cups vegetable broth
- 1 teaspoon dried basil
- 1 teaspoon dried oregano
- Salt and pepper to taste
- 2 tablespoons olive oil
- Grated Parmesan cheese for serving

Method: *(Servings: 6-8).*

1. In the Crock Pot, combine ditalini pasta, cannellini beans, diced tomatoes, diced celery, diced carrots, chopped onion, minced garlic, vegetable broth, dried basil, and dried oregano.
2. Season with salt and pepper. Drizzle olive oil over the ingredients. Stir well.
3. Cover and cook on low for 5 hours or until the pasta and vegetables are tender.
4. Before serving, sprinkle with grated Parmesan cheese. Adjust seasoning if necessary.

Per serving:

Calories: 195; fat: 6g; carb: 30g; protein: 7g

Bacon Ranch Chicken Pasta

Ingredients: *(Time: 6 hours 10 minutes)*

- 3 boneless skinless chicken breasts

- 12 strips bacon (cooked and crumbled)
- 1 tsp minced garlic
- 1 packet dry ranch dressing mix (1 oz packet)
- 1 cup chicken broth
- 2 cups heavy whipping cream
- 16 oz. rotini pasta (cooked to al dente)
- 2 cups cheddar cheese (shredded)

Method: (Servings: 8).

1. Place the chicken, bacon, garlic, ranch mix and chicken broth in a crock pot.
2. Cover and cook on low for 6-8 hours or on high for 3-4 hours.
3. Shred the chicken and return back to the crock pot.
4. Then stir in the heavy whipping cream, pasta and cheddar cheese. Cover and let sit for a few minutes to allow the cheese to melt.
5. Serve immediately while warm and enjoy!

Per serving:

Calories: 713; fat: 47g; carb: 19g; protein: 52g

Creamy Sun Dried Tomato Chicken Pasta

Ingredients: (Time: 6 hours 10 minutes)

- 4 boneless skinless chicken breasts
- 2 cups chicken broth
- 1 teaspoon salt
- 1 teaspoon pepper
- 2 Tablespoons basil dried
- ½ cup sun dried tomatoes in olive oil
- 2 cups heavy cream
- 16 oz angel hair pasta cooked

- 1/2 cup grated parmesan cheese

Method: *(Servings: 4-6).*

1. Place the chicken in the slow cooker. Pour chicken stock on top.
2. Season with salt, pepper, and basil. Pour sun dried tomatoes on top.
3. Cook on low 6-8 hours or until chicken is tender. 6.5 minutes before serving, stir in the heavy cream.
4. After it is combined, stir in the grated parmesan cheese and the angel hair pasta. Serve immediately.

Per serving:

Calories: 635; fat: 29g; carb: 27g; protein: 64g

Easy Italian Spaghetti

Ingredients: *(Time: 2-4 hours)*

- 1-pound ground beef, browned
- 1 (16-ounce) jar marinara sauce
- 1 cup water 8 ounces uncooked pasta
- 1/2 cup grated Parmesan cheese

Method: *(Servings: 4).*

1. Add ground beef, marinara sauce, and water to a greased 4- to 5-quart slow cooker.
2. Cook on high for 2 hours or on low for 4 hours.
3. Forty-five minutes prior to serving, stir dry pasta into meat sauce. The pasta will cook in the sauce.
4. Serve with Parmesan cheese sprinkled on top.

Per serving:

Calories: 556, fat: 18g, carbs: 57g, protein: 36g

Garlic and Artichoke Pasta

Ingredients: *(Time: 3-4 hours)*

- 2 (14 1/2-ounce) cans diced tomatoes with basil, oregano, and garlic
- 2 (14-ounce) cans artichoke hearts, drained and quartered
- 6 cloves garlic, minced
- 1/2 cup heavy cream
- 3 cups cooked pasta

Method: *(Servings: 6).*

1. Pour tomatoes, artichokes, and garlic into a 4- to 5-quart slow cooker.
2. Cook on high for 3–4 hours or on low for 6 –8 hours.
3. Twenty minutes prior to serving, stir in cream.
4. Serve over hot pasta.

Per serving:

Calories: 286, fat: 8g, carbs: 40g, protein: 10g

Creamy Chicken Pasta

Ingredients: *(Time: 4-6 hours 40 minutes)*

- ¼ cup water

- 2 tablespoons arrowroot flour
- 2 pounds boneless, skinless chicken breasts or thighs
- 1 (28-ounce) can no-salt-added diced tomatoes, plus more as needed
- 1 green or red bell pepper, seeded and diced

- 1 small red onion, diced

- 2 garlic cloves, minced
- 1 teaspoon dried oregano
- 1 teaspoon dried parsley
- 1 teaspoon sea salt
- ½ teaspoon freshly ground black pepper
- 8 ounces dried pasta
- 1 cup low-sodium chicken broth (optional)

Method: (Servings: 4).

1. In a small bowl, whisk together the water and arrowroot flour until the flour dissolves.
2. In a slow cooker, combine the chicken, tomatoes, bell pepper, onion, garlic, oregano, parsley, salt, black pepper, and arrowroot mixture. Stir to mix well.
3. Cover the cooker and cook for 4 to 6 hours on Low heat.
4. Stir in the pasta, making sure it is completely submerged. If it is not, add an additional 1 cup of diced tomatoes or 1 cup of chicken broth.
5. Replace the cover on the cooker and cook for 15 to 30 minutes on Low heat, or until the pasta is tender.

Per serving:

Calories: 497; fat: 6g; carbs: 60g; protein: 55g

Greek Chicken Pasta Casserole

Ingredients: (Time: 4-6 hours 15 minutes)

- 2 pounds boneless, skinless chicken thighs or breasts, cut into 1-inch pieces
- 8 ounces dried rotini pasta
- 7 cups low-sodium chicken broth
- ½ red onion, diced
- 3 garlic cloves, minced

- ¼ cup whole Kalamata olives, pitted
- 3 Roma tomatoes, diced
- 2 tablespoons red wine vinegar
- 1 teaspoon extra-virgin olive oil
- 2 teaspoons dried oregano
- 1 teaspoon sea salt
- ½ teaspoon freshly ground black pepper
- ¼ cup crumbled feta cheese

Method: (Servings: 4).

1. In a slow cooker, combine the chicken, pasta, chicken broth, onion, garlic, olives, tomatoes, vinegar, olive oil, oregano, salt, and pepper. Stir to mix well.
2. Cover the cooker and cook for 4 to 6 hours on Low heat.
3. Garnish with the feta cheese for serving.

Per serving:

Calories: 559; fat: 22g; Carbs: 50g; Protein: 46g

Rigatoni with Lamb Meatballs

Ingredients: (Time: 3-5 hours 15 minutes)

- 8 ounces dried rigatoni pasta
- 2 (28-ounce) cans no-salt crushed tomatoes
- 1 small onion, diced
- 1 bell pepper, any color, seeded and diced
- 3 garlic cloves, minced, divided
- 1-pound raw ground lamb
- 1 large egg
- 2 tablespoons bread crumbs
- 1 tablespoon dried parsley

- 1 teaspoon dried oregano
- 1 teaspoon sea salt
- ½ teaspoon freshly ground black pepper

Method: (Servings: 4).

1. In a slow cooker, combine the pasta, tomatoes, onion, bell pepper, and 1 clove of garlic. Stir to mix well.
2. In a large bowl, mix together the ground lamb, egg, bread crumbs, the remaining 2 garlic cloves, parsley, oregano, salt, and black pepper until all of the ingredients are evenly blended.
3. Shape the meat mixture into 6 to 9 large meatballs. Nestle the meatballs into the pasta and tomato sauce.
4. Cover the cooker and cook for 3 to 5 hours on Low heat, or until the pasta is tender.

Per serving:

Calories: 653; fat: 29g; carbs: 69g; protein: 32g

Minestrone Casserole with Italian Sausage

Ingredients: (Time: 4-6 hours 40 minutes)

- 8 ounces Italian-style smoked sausage links, cut into 1-inch pieces
- 1 (28-ounce) can no-salt-added diced tomatoes
- 1 cup low-sodium vegetable broth
- 1 (15-ounce) can reduced-sodium chickpeas, drained and rinsed
- 3 celery stalks, diced
- 3 carrots, diced
- 1 onion, diced
- 4 garlic cloves, minced
- 8 ounces' green beans, cut into 1-inch pieces

- 2 zucchinis, diced
- 1 tablespoon Italian seasoning
- 1 teaspoon sea salt
- ½ teaspoon freshly ground black pepper
- ¼ teaspoon ground cumin
- 2 bay leaves
- 4 ounces' elbow macaroni
- ⅓ cup grated
- Parmesan cheese Fresh parsley, for garnish

Method: (Servings: 4).

1. In a slow cooker, combine the sausage, tomatoes, vegetable broth, chickpeas, celery, carrots, onion, garlic, green beans, zucchini, Italian seasoning, salt, pepper, cumin, and bay leaves. Stir to mix well.
2. Cover the cooker and cook for 4 to 6 hours on Low heat.
3. Remove and discard the bay leaves.
4. Stir in the macaroni and Parmesan cheese. Replace the cover on the cooker and cook for 30 minutes on Low heat, or until the macaroni is tender.
5. Garnish with fresh parsley for serving.

Per serving:

Calories: 567; fat: 22g; carbs: 73g; protein: 25g

Herbed Fish Casserole with Rice

Ingredients: (Time: 2-4 hours 10 minutes)

- Non-stick cooking spray
- 1 cup raw long-grain brown rice, rinsed
- 2½ cups low-sodium chicken broth
- 1 tablespoon freshly squeezed lemon juice

- 2 garlic cloves, minced
- 1 teaspoon sea salt
- 1 teaspoon dried oregano
- 1 teaspoon dried parsley
- 1 teaspoon dried basil
- 1 teaspoon dried thyme
- ½ teaspoon onion powder
- ½ teaspoon freshly ground black pepper
- 1-pound fresh cod fillets

Method: *(Servings: 4).*

1. Generously coat a slow cooker insert with cooking spray.
2. Put the rice, chicken broth, lemon juice, garlic, salt, oregano, parsley, basil, thyme, onion powder, and pepper in a slow cooker, and stir to mix well.
3. Place the cod fillets on top of the rice mixture.
4. Cover the cooker and cook for 2 to 4 hours on Low heat.

Per serving:

Calories: 296; fat: 3g; carbs: 38g; protein: 31g

Chicken Casserole with Rice

Ingredients: *(Time: 3-5 hours 15 minutes)*

- Non-stick cooking spray
- 1 cup raw long-grain brown rice, rinsed
- 2½ cups low-sodium chicken broth
- 1 small onion, diced
- 4 garlic cloves, minced
- 1 teaspoon extra-virgin olive oil
- 2 Roma tomatoes, chopped

- 4 ounces whole Kalamata olives, pitted
- 2 tablespoons drained capers
- 1 teaspoon sea salt
- 1 teaspoon ground cumin
- ½ teaspoon freshly ground black pepper
- 1½ pounds bone-in, skin-on chicken thighs
- 1 lemon, thinly sliced
- ¼ cup chopped fresh basil
- ¼ cup crumbled feta cheese

Method: *(Servings: 4).*

1. Generously coat a slow-cooker insert with cooking spray.
2. Put the rice, chicken broth, onion, garlic, olive oil, tomatoes, olives, capers, salt, cumin, and pepper in a slow cooker. Stir to mix well.
3. Nestle the chicken thighs into the rice mixture and top with lemon slices.
4. Cover the cooker and cook for 3 to 5 hours on Low heat.
5. Garnish with the fresh basil and feta for serving.

Per serving:

Calories: 684; fat: 39g; carbs: 49g; protein: 37g

Chicken Artichoke Rice Bake

Ingredients: *(Time: 3-5 hours 10 minutes)*

- Non-stick cooking spray
- 1 cup raw long-grain brown rice, rinsed
- 2½ cups low-sodium chicken broth
- 1 (14-ounce) can artichoke hearts, drained and rinsed
- ½ small onion, diced
- 2 garlic cloves, minced

- 10 ounces' fresh spinach, chopped
- 1 teaspoon dried thyme
- ½ teaspoon sea salt
- ½ teaspoon freshly ground black pepper
- 1 pound boneless, skinless chicken breast

Method: (Servings: 4).

1. Generously coat a slow-cooker insert with cooking spray.
2. Put the rice, chicken broth, artichoke hearts, onion, garlic, spinach, thyme, salt, and pepper in a slow cooker. Gently stir to mix well.
3. Place the chicken on top of the rice mixture.
4. Cover the cooker and cook for 3 to 5 hours on Low heat.
5. Remove the chicken from the cooker, shred it, and stir it back into the rice in the cooker.

Per serving:

Calories: 323; fat: 4g; carbs: 44g; protein: 32g

Rice with Blackened Fish

Ingredients: (Time: 2-4 hours 40 minutes)

- 1 teaspoon (or more) of red pepper flakes to the blackening seasoning.
- 1 teaspoon ground cumin
- 1 teaspoon ground coriander
- 1 teaspoon garlic powder
- 1 teaspoon paprika
- ½ teaspoon sea salt
- ½ teaspoon freshly ground black pepper
- ½ teaspoon onion powder
- 1 pound fresh salmon fillets

- 1 cup raw long-grain brown rice, rinsed
- 2½ cups low-sodium chicken broth
- ¼ cup diced tomato

Method: *(Servings: 4).*

1. In a small bowl, stir together the cumin, coriander, garlic powder, paprika, salt, pepper, and onion powder.
2. Generously season the salmon fillets with the blackening seasoning.
3. In a slow cooker, combine the rice, chicken broth, and tomato. Stir to mix well.
4. Place the seasoned salmon on top of the rice mixture.
5. Cover the cooker and cook for 2 to 4 hours on Low heat.

Per serving:

Calories: 318; fat: 6g; carbs: 38g; protein: 29g

Rice with Pork Chops

Ingredients: *(Time: 3-5 hours 10 minutes)*

- 1 cup raw long-grain brown rice, rinsed
- 2½ cups low-sodium chicken broth
- 1 cup sliced tomato
- 8 ounces' fresh spinach, chopped
- 1 small onion, chopped
- 2 garlic cloves, minced
- 2 teaspoons dried oregano
- 2 teaspoons dried basil
- 1 teaspoon sea salt
- ½ teaspoon freshly ground black pepper
- 4 thick-cut pork chops
- ¼ cup grated Parmesan cheese

Method: *(Servings: 4).*

1. In a slow cooker, combine the rice, chicken broth, tomato, spinach, onion, garlic, oregano, basil, salt, and pepper. Stir to mix well.
2. Place the pork chops on top of the rice mixture.
3. Cover the cooker and cook for 3 to 5 hours on Low heat.
4. Top with the Parmesan cheese for serving.

Per serving:

Calories: 375; fat: 10g; carbs: 43gprotein: 31g

Mediterranean "Fried" Rice

Ingredients: *(Time: 3-5 hours 15 minutes)*

- Nonstick cooking spray
- 1 cup raw long-grain brown rice, rinsed
- 2½ cups low-sodium chicken broth
- 2 tablespoons extra-virgin olive oil
- 2 tablespoons balsamic vinegar
- 2 zucchinis, diced
- 4 ounces' mushrooms, diced
- 1 small onion, diced
- 2 garlic cloves, minced
- 1 carrot, diced
- 1 bell pepper, any color, seeded and diced
- ¼ cup peas (raw, frozen, or canned)
- 1 teaspoon sea salt
- 1 pound boneless, skinless chicken breast, cut into ½-inch pieces
- 2 large eggs

Method: *(Servings: 4).*

1. Generously coat a slow-cooker insert with cooking spray.
1. Put the rice, chicken broth, olive oil, vinegar, zucchini, mushrooms, onion, garlic, carrot, bell pepper, peas, and salt in a slow cooker. Stir to mix well.
2. Nestle the chicken into the rice mixture.
3. Cover the cooker and cook for 3 to 5 hours on Low heat.
4. In a small bowl, whisk the eggs. Pour the eggs over the chicken and rice.
5. Replace the cover on the cooker and cook for 15 to 30 minutes on Low heat, or until the eggs are scrambled and cooked through.
6. Fluff the rice with a fork before serving.

Per serving:

Calories: 431; fat: 14g; carbos: 48g; protein: 35g

Easy Chicken and Rice

Ingredients: (Time: 3-5 hours 10 minutes)

- 1 cup raw long-grain brown rice, rinsed
- 2½ cups low-sodium chicken broth
- 1 small onion, diced
- 2 garlic cloves, minced
- 1 teaspoon dried oregano
- 1 teaspoon dried parsley
- 1 teaspoon sea salt
- ½ teaspoon freshly ground black pepper
- 1½ pounds bone-in, skin-on chicken thighs

Method: (Servings: 4).

1. In a slow cooker, combine the rice, chicken broth, onion, garlic, oregano, parsley, salt, and pepper. Stir to mix well.
2. Nestle the chicken on top of the rice mixture.

3. Cover the cooker and cook for 3 to 5 hours on Low heat.

Per serving:

Calories: 546; fat: 27g; carbs: 38g; protein: 35g

Lemon Rice Pilaf

Ingredients: *(Time: 3-5 hours 40 minutes)*

- 1 cup raw long-grain brown rice, rinsed
- 2½ cups low-sodium vegetable broth
- Juice of 2 lemons
- 1 teaspoon grated lemon zest
- 1 small onion, diced
- 2 garlic cloves, minced
- 1 teaspoon sea salt
- 1 teaspoon dried dill
- 2 tablespoons fresh parsley

Method: *(Servings: 4).*

1. In a slow cooker, combine the rice, vegetable broth, lemon juice, lemon zest, onion, garlic, salt, and dill. Stir to mix well.
2. Cover the cooker and cook for 3 to 5 hours on Low heat.
3. Garnish with the fresh parsley for serving.

Per serving:

Calories: 186; fat: 2g; carbs: 40g; protein: 6g

Mediterranean Rice and Sausage

Ingredients: *(Time: 8 hours 15 minutes)*

- 1½ pounds Italian sausage, crumbled
- 1 medium onion, chopped
- 2 tablespoons steak sauce
- 2 cups long grain rice, uncooked
- 1 (14-ounce) can diced tomatoes with juice
- ½ cup water
- 1 medium green pepper, diced

Method: *(Servings: 6).*

1. Spray your slow cooker with olive oil or non-stick cooking spray.
2. Add the sausage, onion, and steak sauce to the slow cooker.
3. Cook on low for 8 to 10 hours.
4. After 8 hours, add the rice, tomatoes, water and green pepper. Stir to combine thoroughly.
5. Cook an additional 20 to 25 minutes or until the rice is cooked.

Per serving

Calories 650, fat 36 g, carbs 57 g, protein 22 g

Brown Rice Pudding

Ingredients: *(Time: 3 hours 5 minutes)*

- 4 cups milk of your choice
- ¼ cup maple syrup
- ⅔ cup brown rice
- 1 cinnamon stick
- 1 teaspoon vanilla

Method: *(Servings: 4-6).*

1. Spray your slow cooker with nonstick cooking spray.

2. Add all the ingredients to the slow cooker and stir.
3. Cook on high for 3 hours.
4. Remove the cinnamon stick and serve.

Per serving

Calories 210, fat 1 g, carbs 42.4 g, protein 7.8 g

Fish & Seafood

Cioppino

Ingredients: (Time: 5 hours 10 minutes)

- 1 (15-ounce) can diced tomatoes, undrained
- 1 red bell pepper, chopped
- 2 medium onions, chopped
- 3 celery stalks, chopped
- 2 cups seafood/fish stock
- 6 ounces' tomato paste
- ½ cup white wine (or additional seafood stock)
- 1 tablespoon garlic, minced
- 2 teaspoons Italian seasoning
- 1 teaspoon sugar
- 1 bay leaf
- ¾ teaspoon crushed red pepper flakes (optional)
- 12 ounces' solid white albacore in water, drained
- 1 pound cooked shrimp, peeled and deveined
- 12 ounces lump crabmeat, drained
- 6 ounces chopped clams, drained
- 2 tablespoons fresh basil, chopped
- 1 tablespoon fresh parsley, chopped
- Salt and pepper, to taste

Method: (Servings: 6-8).

1. Spray your slow cooker with olive oil.
2. Place the following ingredients into the slow cooker: tomatoes, pepper, onions, celery, seafood stock, tomato paste, white wine, garlic, Italian seasoning, sugar, bay leaf, and red pepper flakes.
3. Cook on low for 4–6 hours. Add the tuna, shrimp, crabmeat, and clams.

4. Stir until well combined, then cook for about another 10 minutes.
5. When the seafood has heated, add the basil and parsley.

Per serving

Calories 237, fat 5 g, carbs 10 g, protein 33 g

Shrimp Scampi

Ingredients: *(Time: 1 hours 40 minutes)*

- ⅓ cup chicken broth
- 2 tablespoons olive oil
- 2 tablespoons butter
- 1 tablespoon minced garlic
- 2 tablespoons parsley or
- 2 teaspoons dried
- ½ freshly squeezed lemon
- Salt and pepper, to taste
- 1 ½ pounds raw shrimp, peeled & deveined

Method: *(Servings: 4).*

1. Add everything but the shrimp to the slow cooker and stir to combine.
2. Mix in the raw shrimp.
3. Cook on high for 1½ hours.
4. Serve with pasta or a nice crunchy Italian bread.

Per serving

Calories 340, fat 19.5 g, carbs 2 g, protein 36.8 g

Tilapia Pesto

Ingredients: *(Time: 2-4 hours 10 minutes)*

- 1 cup pesto
- 4 tilapia fillets

- ¼ cup tomato paste
- 1 cup onion, diced
- 1 teaspoon salt
- ½ teaspoon black pepper
- 1 medium lemon, sliced

Method: *(Servings: 4).*

1. Cook the fillets in four separate foil packets, so lay a sheet (or four) of aluminum foil on the countertop.
2. Spread ¼ cup of pesto in the center of each sheet of foil.
3. Place 1 fillet on top of each layer of pesto.
4. Spread 1 tablespoon of tomato paste across each fillet.
5. Place ¼ cup onion over the tomato paste. Salt and pepper each fillet to taste. Place a couple of slices of lemon over each fillet. Seal the foil packets by folding tightly.
6. Now you can place the packets into freezer bags and freeze or cook immediately. If cooking now, cook on low for 2 hours. If cooking from frozen, cook on low for 4 hours.

Per serving

Calories 420, fat 28 g, carbs 9 g, protein 32 g

Seafood Stew

Ingredients: *(Time: 5 hours 10 minutes)*

- 1¾ pounds crushed tomatoes
- 4 cups vegetable broth
- ½ cup white wine
- 3 cloves garlic, minced
- 1 pound
- Dutch baby potatoes or other white/yellow baby potatoes, cut into bite-sized pieces
- ½ medium onion, diced (about ½ cup)
- 1 teaspoon dried thyme
- 1 teaspoon dried basil
- 1 teaspoon dried cilantro
- ½ teaspoon celery salt
- ½ teaspoon salt
- ½ teaspoon pepper
- ¼ teaspoon red pepper flakes
- Pinch cayenne pepper
- 2 pounds' seafood (scallops, extra-large shrimp and crab legs)

Method: (Servings: 4-6).

1. Add everything except the seafood to your slow cooker.
2. Cook on high for 2 hours or low for 4 hours.
3. Add the seafood to the slow cooker and cook for an additional 30 to 60 minutes or until the seafood is fully cooked.
4. Serve and enjoy.

Per serving

Calories 236, fat 1 g, carbs 31 g, protein 22 g,

Lemon Dill Salmon

Ingredients: (Time: 1 hours 10 minutes)

1-pound salmon fillet, cut into 4 portions

Salt and pepper

Juice from 2 lemons

2 sprigs fresh dill, finely chopped

Method: *(Servings: 4-6).*

1. Line your slow cooker with a large sheet of parchment paper.
2. Lay the salmon flat on top of the parchment paper. Try not to overlap the pieces. You may have to cut the fillets into smaller pieces to get them to fit.
3. Sprinkle the fillets with salt and pepper and dill, then squeeze on the lemon juice.
4. Cook on high for about an hour or until the salmon is flaky.
5. Carefully lift the parchment paper out of the slow cooker and transfer the salmon to a serving dish.

Per serving

Calories 168, fat 7.1 g, carbs 3.2 g, protein 22.3 g

Seafood Paella

Ingredients: *(Time: 2 hours 10 minutes)*

- 1 teaspoon extra-virgin olive oil
- 1½ pounds boneless skinless chicken breasts, cubed
- ½ pound sliced chorizo
- Kosher salt and freshly ground black pepper, to taste
- 1 cup uncooked long-grain rice
- 1 (15-ounce) can diced tomatoes, undrained
- 1 large yellow onion, peeled and chopped
- 4 cloves garlic, peeled and minced
- 2 teaspoons paprika

- ¼ teaspoon cayenne pepper
- 2 cups reduced-sodium chicken broth
- ⅓ cup dry white wine
- ½ pound raw medium shrimp, peeled and deveined
- 1½ cups frozen peas, thawed and drained
- Fresh parsley, chopped, for garnish
- Lemon wedges, for serving

Method: (Servings: 6).

1. In a large skillet, heat olive oil over medium-high heat. When the skillet is hot, add the chicken and chorizo.
2. Cook until chicken is brown and chorizo is cooked.
3. Transfer the chicken and chorizo to the slow cooker and sprinkle with salt and pepper.
4. Add the uncooked rice, tomatoes, onion, garlic, and all of the spices, followed by the chicken broth and wine. Stir a couple of times to mix well.
5. Cook on high for an hour and a half, then add the shrimp and the peas. Stir those in, then cook for 30 more minutes.
6. Serve when the shrimp is cooked through.

Per serving

Calories 274, fat 11 g, carbs 22 g, protein 21.7 g

Garlic Lemon Shrimp

Ingredients: (Time: 2 hours 15 minutes)

- 1½ lbs large shrimp, peeled and deveined
- 4 cloves garlic, minced
- ¼ cup fresh parsley, chopped
- 1/3 cup olive oil

- ¼ cup fresh lemon juice
- 1 teaspoon dried oregano
- Salt and pepper to taste

Method: *(Servings: 6).*

1. In a bowl, mix together garlic, parsley, olive oil, lemon juice, oregano, salt, and pepper.
2. Place the shrimp in the crock pot and pour the mixture over them, ensuring they are well-coated.
3. Cover and cook on low for 2 hours, stirring occasionally.
4. Serve over cooked rice or with crusty bread to soak up the delicious sauce.

Per serving

Calories: 154; fat: 15g; carb: 6g; protein: 1g

Mediterranean Herb-Roasted Cod

Ingredients: *(Time: 3 hours 20 minutes)*

- 2 lbs cod fillets
- ¼ cup fresh basil, chopped
- ¼ cup fresh dill, chopped
- ¼ cup fresh mint, chopped
- 1/3 cup olive oil
- 3 cloves garlic, minced
- 1 lemon, sliced
- Salt and pepper to taste

Method: *(Servings: 4-6).*

1. Mix together basil, dill, mint, olive oil, and garlic in a bowl.

2. Place cod fillets in the crock pot, season with salt and pepper, and pour the herb mixture over them.
3. Arrange lemon slices on top, cover, and cook on low for 3 hours.
4. Serve with a side of roasted vegetables or a Greek salad.

Per serving

Calories: 277; fat: 16g; carb: 2g; protein: 30g

Lemon Garlic Butter Scallops

Ingredients: *(Time: 2 hours 45 minutes)*

- 1 ½ lbs fresh scallops
- ½ cup unsalted butter, melted
- 4 cloves garlic, minced
- Zest of 1 lemon
- ¼ cup fresh parsley, chopped
- Salt and pepper to taste

Method: *(Servings: 4-6).*

1. Rinse and pat dry the scallops; place them in the crock pot.
2. In a bowl, mix melted butter, minced garlic, lemon zest, parsley, salt, and pepper.
3. Pour the butter mixture over the scallops, ensuring they are evenly coated.
4. Cover and cook on low for 2.5 hours. Serve over a bed of couscous or quinoa.

Per serving

Calories: 216; fat: 13g; carb: 7g; protein: 18g

Mediterranean Sardine Stew

Ingredients: *(Time: 3 hours 20 minutes)*

- 1 pound fresh sardines, cleaned and scaled
- 1 cup diced onions
- 1 cup diced bell peppers (red and green)
- 1 cup diced zucchini
- 1 cup diced tomatoes
- 2 cloves garlic, minced
- ¼ cup olive oil
- 2 tablespoons tomato paste
- 1 teaspoon dried oregano
- 1 teaspoon dried basil
- Salt and pepper to taste
- Fresh basil leaves for garnish
- Cooked quinoa or couscous for serving

Method: *(Servings: 6).*

1. In your crock pot, combine the fresh sardines, diced onions, diced bell peppers, diced zucchini, diced tomatoes, minced garlic, olive oil, tomato paste, dried oregano, dried basil, salt, and pepper. Stir to combine.
2. Cover and cook on low for 3 hours, or until the sardines are tender and cooked through.
3. Serve over cooked quinoa or couscous, garnished with fresh basil leaves.

Per serving

Calories: 291; fat: 18g; carb: 12g; protein: 21g

Shrimp and Mushroom Risotto

Ingredients: *(Time: 2 hours 45 minutes)*

- 1-pound large shrimp, peeled and deveined
- 2 cups Arborio rice

- 1 cup sliced mushrooms
- 1 cup diced onions
- 2 cloves garlic, minced
- 4 cups chicken broth
- ½ cup dry white wine
- ½ cup grated Parmesan cheese
- 2 tablespoons butter
- Salt and pepper to taste
- Chopped fresh parsley for garnish

Method: (Servings: 4).

1. In your crock pot, combine the shrimp, Arborio rice, sliced mushrooms, diced onions, minced garlic, chicken broth, dry white wine, grated Parmesan cheese, butter, salt, and pepper. Stir to combine.
2. Cover and cook on low for 2.5 hours, or until the rice is tender and the shrimp are cooked through.
3. Serve hot, garnished with chopped fresh parsley.

Per serving

Calories: 746; fat: 42g; carb: 41g; protein: 68g

Mussels with Tomato Sauce

Ingredients: (Time: 2 hours 20 minutes)

- 2 pounds' mussels, cleaned and debearded
- 2 cups diced tomatoes
- 1 cup diced onions
- 1 cup diced bell peppers (red and green)
- 2 cloves garlic, minced
- ¼ cup olive oil

- ¼ cup white wine
- 1 teaspoon dried oregano
- 1 teaspoon dried basil
- Salt and pepper to taste
- Fresh basil leaves for garnish
- Crusty bread for serving

Method: (Servings: 4).

1. In your crock pot, combine the cleaned mussels, diced tomatoes, diced onions, diced bell peppers, minced garlic, olive oil, white wine, dried oregano, dried basil, salt, and pepper.
2. Stir to combine.
3. Cover and cook on low for 2 hours, or until the mussels have opened and are cooked.
4. Serve hot, garnished with fresh basil leaves, and provide crusty bread for soaking up the delicious tomato sauce.

Per serving

Calories: 372; fat: 19g; carb: 21g; protein: 29g

Cajun Catfish Gumbo

Ingredients: (Time: 4 hours 20 minutes)

- 2 pounds' catfish fillets, cut into chunks
- 1 cup diced onions
- 1 cup diced bell peppers (red and green)
- 1 cup diced celery
- 2 cloves garlic, minced
- 1 can (14.5 ounces) diced tomatoes
- 4 cups chicken broth

- ¼ cup all-purpose flour
- ¼ cup vegetable oil
- 2 tablespoons Cajun seasoning
- Salt and pepper to taste
- Cooked rice for serving
- Chopped fresh parsley for garnish

Method: (Servings: 8).

1. In your crock pot, combine the catfish chunks, diced onions, diced bell peppers, diced celery, minced garlic, diced tomatoes, and chicken broth.
2. Stir to combine.
3. In a separate skillet, make a roux by heating the vegetable oil over medium heat and gradually adding the flour while stirring constantly. Cook until the roux is dark brown but not burned.
4. Add the roux to the crock pot mixture and stir well.
5. Season with Cajun seasoning, salt, and pepper. Cover and cook on low for 4 hours.
6. Serve over cooked rice, garnished with chopped fresh parsley.

Per serving

Calories: 399; fat: 18g; carb: 10g; protein: 46g

Creamy Crock Pot Tuna and Spinach Pasta

Ingredients: (Time: 2 hours 45 minutes)

- 12 ounces canned tuna, drained
- 2 cups fresh spinach leaves
- 2 cups cooked pasta
- 1 cup diced tomatoes
- ½ cup diced onions

- 2 cloves garlic, minced
- 1 cup shredded mozzarella cheese
- ¼ cup grated Parmesan cheese
- 1 cup heavy cream
- 2 tablespoons butter
- Salt and pepper to taste
- Fresh basil leaves for garnish

Method: (Servings: 4).

1. In your crock pot, combine the drained tuna, fresh spinach leaves, cooked pasta, diced tomatoes, diced onions, minced garlic, shredded mozzarella cheese, grated Parmesan cheese, heavy cream, butter, salt, and pepper.
2. Stir to combine.
3. Cover and cook on low for 2.5 hours, or until the pasta is heated through, and the cheese is melted and bubbly.

Per serving

Calories: 405; fat: 20g; carb: 27g; protein: 31g

Octopus Salad

Ingredients: (Time: 2 hours 20 minutes)

- 2 pounds' octopus, cleaned and sliced into rings
- 1 cup diced tomatoes
- 1 cup diced cucumbers
- ½ cup diced red onions
- ¼ cup chopped fresh parsley
- 2 cloves garlic, minced
- ¼ cup olive oil
- 2 tablespoons red wine vinegar

- Salt and pepper to taste
- Lemon wedges for garnish

Method: *(Servings: 4).*

1. In your crock pot, combine the octopus's rings, diced tomatoes, diced cucumbers, diced red onions, chopped fresh parsley, minced garlic, olive oil, red wine vinegar, salt, and pepper.
2. Stir to combine.
3. Cover and cook on low for 2 hours, or until the octopus is tender.
4. Serve hot or chilled, garnished with lemon wedges.

Per serving

Calories: 333; fat: 16g; carb: 11g; protein: 35g

Tuna and White Bean Stew

Ingredients: *(Time: 4 hours 15 minutes)*

- 2 cans (5 ounces each) tuna, drained and flaked
- 2 cans (15 ounces each) white beans, drained and rinsed
- 1 cup diced tomatoes
- 1 cup diced onions
- 2 cloves garlic, minced
- ½ cup chicken broth
- ¼ cup olive oil
- 1 teaspoon dried thyme
- Salt and pepper to taste
- Fresh parsley for garnish
- Crusty bread for serving

Method: *(Servings: 6).*

1. In your crock pot, combine the flaked tuna, white beans, diced tomatoes, diced onions, minced garlic, chicken broth, olive oil, dried thyme, salt, and pepper.
2. Stir to combine.
3. Cover and cook on low for 3 hours.
4. Serve hot, garnished with fresh parsley, and provide crusty bread for dipping.

Per serving

Calories: 385; fat: 12g; carb: 42g; protein: 30g

Coconut Curry Mussels

Ingredients: *(Time: 2 hours 15 minutes)*

- 2 pounds mussels, cleaned and debearded
- 1 can (14 ounces) coconut milk
- 2 tablespoons red curry paste
- 1 cup diced tomatoes
- 1 cup diced onions
- 2 cloves garlic, minced
- 1 tablespoon fish sauce
- 1 tablespoon brown sugar
- 1 lime, juiced
- Fresh cilantro leaves for garnish
- Cooked rice or crusty bread for serving

Method: *(Servings: 4).*

1. In your crock pot, combine the cleaned mussels, coconut milk, red curry paste, diced tomatoes, diced onions, minced garlic, fish sauce, and brown sugar.
2. Stir to combine.
3. Cover and cook on LOW for 2 hours, or until the mussels have opened and are cooked.

4. Stir in the lime juice.
5. Serve hot, garnished with fresh cilantro leaves, and provide cooked rice or crusty bread for soaking up the coconut curry sauce.

Per serving

Calories: 662; fat: 36g; carb: 36f; protein: 51g

Herbed Tuna Steaks

Ingredients: *(Time: 4-6 hours 10 minutes)*

- Non-stick cooking spray
- 4 (1-inch-thick) fresh tuna steaks
- 1 teaspoon sea salt ¼ teaspoon freshly ground black pepper
- 2 teaspoons extra-virgin olive oil 2 teaspoons dried thyme
- 2 teaspoons dried rosemary

Method: *(Servings: 6).*

1. Coat a slow-cooker insert with cooking spray, or line the bottom and sides with parchment paper or aluminum foil.
2. Season the tuna steaks all over with salt and pepper and place them in the prepared slow cooker in a single layer.
3. Drizzle with the olive oil and sprinkle with the thyme and rosemary.
4. Cover the cooker and cook for 4 to 6 hours on Low heat.

Per serving

Calories: 339; fat: 5g; carbs: 1g; protein: 68g

Sesame-Ginger Cod

Ingredients: *(Time: 4-6 hours 10 minutes)*

- ¼ cup low-sodium soy sauce
- 2 tablespoons balsamic vinegar
- 1 tablespoon freshly squeezed lemon juice
- 2 teaspoons extra-virgin olive oil
- 1 tablespoon ground ginger
- ½ teaspoon sea salt
- ¼ teaspoon freshly ground black pepper
- Non-stick cooking spray
- 2 pounds' fresh cod fillets
- ½ teaspoon sesame seeds
- 4 scallions, green parts only, cut into 3-inch lengths

Method: (Servings: 4).

1. In a small bowl, whisk together the soy sauce, vinegar, lemon juice, olive oil, ginger, salt, and pepper until combined. Set aside.
2. Coat a slow-cooker insert with cooking spray and place the cod in the prepared slow cooker. Pour the soy sauce mixture over the cod. Cover the cooker and cook for 4 to 6 hours on Low heat.
3. Garnish with sesame seeds and scallions for serving.

Per serving:

Calories: 282; fat: 4g; carbos: 4g; protein: 52g

Italian Baccalà

Ingredients: (Time: 8 hours)

- 1½ pounds salt cod

- 1 (15-ounce) can no-salt-added diced tomatoes
- ½ onion, chopped
- 2 garlic cloves, minced

- ½ teaspoon red pepper flakes
- ¼ cup chopped fresh parsley, plus more for garnish
- Juice of ½ lemon

Method: (Servings: 4).

1. Wash the salt cod to remove any visible salt. Completely submerge the cod in a large bowl of water and let it soak for at least 2 to 3 hours.
2. If you are soaking it for longer than 24 hours, change the water after 12 hours.
3. In a slow cooker, combine the tomatoes, onion, garlic, red pepper flakes, parsley, and lemon juice. Stir to mix well. Drain the cod and add it to the slow cooker, breaking it apart as necessary to make it fit.
4. Cover the cooker and cook for 4 to 6 hours on Low heat.
5. Garnish with the remaining fresh parsley for serving.

Per serving:

Calories: 211; fat: 2g; carbs: 8g; protein: 39g

Poultry

Chicken Shawarma Wraps

Ingredients: (Time: 4-6 hours 15 minutes)

- 1 small onion, sliced
- 2 pounds boneless, skinless chicken thighs, cut into 1½-inch-thick strips
- 3 tablespoons white vinegar
- 3 tablespoons freshly squeezed lemon juice
- 2 tablespoons extra-virgin olive oil
- 1 tablespoon water
- 3 garlic cloves, minced
- 2 teaspoons ground allspice
- 1 teaspoon sea salt
- 1 teaspoon ground nutmeg
- 1 teaspoon ground cardamom
- 1 teaspoon garlic powder
- ½ teaspoon freshly ground black pepper
- ½ teaspoon za'atar (optional)
- ¼ teaspoon ground cinnamon
- ¼ cup fresh parsley, minced
- 4 large pita breads

Method: (Servings: 4).

1. Put the onion in a slow cooker and top it with the chicken.
2. In a small bowl, whisk together the vinegar, lemon juice, olive oil, water, garlic, allspice, salt, nutmeg, cardamom, garlic powder, pepper, za'atar (if using), and cinnamon until blended. Pour the sauce into the slow cooker. Stir to mix well.
3. Cover the cooker and cook for 4 to 6 hours on Low heat.
4. Sprinkle the parsley over the chicken and serve the chicken in the pitas.

5. If you like, garnish this shawarma with diced tomato, red onion, cucumber, and tahini or tzatziki sauce.

Per serving:

Calories: 509; fat: 22g; carbs: 39g; protein: 38g

Sweet and Tangy Duck

Ingredients: (Time: 3-4 hours 5 minutes)

- 1 (3-pound) duckling, skin removed
- 1 tablespoon olive oil
- 1/2 teaspoon kosher salt
- 1/2 teaspoon freshly ground black pepper
- 1/2 teaspoon red pepper flakes
- 2 cloves garlic, minced
- 1 medium Granny Smith apple, peeled, cored, and cut into 1" pieces
- 1 medium pear, peeled, cored, and cut into 1" pieces
- 1 tablespoon lemon juice
- 1 large red onion, peeled and chopped
- 1 large carrot, peeled and chopped
- 1 stalk celery, chopped
- 1/2 cup dry red wine
- 1/4 cup honey
- 1/4 cup cider vinegar
- 1 cup Roasted Chicken Broth

Method: (Servings: 6).

1. Remove any extraneous fat from the duck. Cut into serving-size portions.
2. Heat olive oil in a large skillet or Dutch oven until hot but not smoking. Add the duck and season with salt, pepper, and red pepper flakes.

3. Cook for 3 minutes on one side. Add garlic to the pan, flip the duck, and cook for 1 minute. While duck is browning, place apple and pear pieces in a bowl of cold water with lemon juice to keep from browning while prepping the vegetables.
4. Place onion, carrot, and celery in the bottom of a 4- to 5-quart slow cooker. Drain the apple and pear, and top vegetables with the duck and apple and pear mixture.
5. In a small bowl, whisk the wine, honey, vinegar, and broth together. Pour over the duck. Cover and cook on high for 3 –4 hours.

Per serving:

Calories: 422, fat: 12g, carbs: 26g, protein: 46

Chicken with Lemon and Artichokes

Ingredients: (Time: 6-8 hours 10 minutes)

- 2 pounds' bone-in, skin-on chicken thighs
- 1 large onion, sliced
- 1 (15-ounce) can artichoke hearts, drained, rinsed, and chopped
- ¼ cup freshly squeezed lemon juice
- 1 tablespoon extra-virgin olive oil
- 3 garlic cloves, minced
- 2 teaspoons dried thyme
- 1 teaspoon sea salt
- ½ teaspoon freshly ground black pepper
- 1 lemon, thinly sliced

Method: (Servings: 4).

1. In a slow cooker, combine the chicken and onion. Top with the artichoke hearts.
2. In a small bowl, whisk together the lemon juice, olive oil, garlic, thyme, salt, and pepper. Pour the sauce into the slow cooker. Top the chicken with lemon slices.
3. Cover the cooker and cook for 6 to 8 hours on Low heat.

4. Serve this recipe with your preferred cooked rice —whether it is brown rice or "rice" made from cauliflower.

Per serving:

Calories: 558; fat: 38g; carbs: 13g; protein: 41g

Citrusy and Sticky Honey Wings

Ingredients: *(Time: 6-7 hours 10 minutes)*

- 3 pounds' chicken wings, tips removed
- 1/4 cup honey
- 1/4 cup orange juice
- 1 tablespoon lime juice
- 1 teaspoon sea salt, crushed in a mortar and pestle
- 1 teaspoon freshly ground black pepper
- 1/4 teaspoon garlic powder
- 1/4 teaspoon onion powder

Method: *(Servings: 10).*

1. Place the wings into a 4- to 5-quart slow cooker.
2. In a small bowl, whisk the honey, orange juice, lime juice, salt, pepper, garlic powder, and onion powder.
3. Pour over the wings. Toss to coat with sauce.
4. Cook for 6–7 hours on low. Stir before serving.

Per serving:

Calories: 328, fat: 21g, carbs: 8g, protein: 24g

Greek Chicken Casserole

Ingredients: (Time: 6-8 hours 15 minutes)

- 3 pounds boneless, skinless chicken thighs
- 1 small onion, chopped
- 4 Roma tomatoes, chopped
- 1 (12-ounce) jar artichoke hearts, drained
- 1 cup sliced pitted Kalamata olives
- 1 tablespoon dried oregano
- 1 teaspoon sea salt
- ½ teaspoon freshly ground black pepper
- ½ cup low-sodium chicken broth
- 1 tablespoon extra-virgin olive oil
- 1 lemon, thinly sliced
- ¾ cup crumbled feta cheese
- 2 tablespoons chopped fresh parsley

Method: (Servings: 6).

1. Place the chicken in the bottom of a slow cooker.
2. Add the onion, tomatoes, artichoke hearts, olives, oregano, salt, and pepper.
3. In a small bowl, whisk together the chicken broth and olive oil to combine. Pour the liquid over the chicken and vegetables and top with the lemon slices.
4. Cover the cooker and cook for 6 to 8 hours on Low heat.
5. Garnish with feta and fresh parsley for serving.

Per serving:

Calories: 405; fat: 24g; carbs: 13g; protein: 37g

Tuscan Turkey

Ingredients: (Time: 4-8 hours 15 minutes)

- 1 pound new potatoes, halved
- 1 red bell pepper, seeded and sliced
- 1 small onion, sliced
- 4 boneless, skinless turkey breast fillets (about 2 pounds)
- 1 cup low-sodium chicken broth ½ cup grated Parmesan cheese
- 3 garlic cloves, minced
- 1 teaspoon dried oregano
- 1 teaspoon dried rosemary
- ½ teaspoon sea salt
- ½ teaspoon freshly ground black pepper
- ½ teaspoon dried thyme
- ¼ cup chopped fresh basil

Method: *(Servings: 4).*

1. In a slow cooker, combine the potatoes, bell pepper, and onion. Stir to mix well.
2. Place the turkey on top of the vegetables.
3. In a small bowl, whisk together the chicken broth, Parmesan cheese, garlic, oregano, rosemary, salt, black pepper, and thyme until blended. Pour the sauce over the turkey.
4. Cover the cooker and cook for 6 to 8 hours on Low heat. 5.Garnish with fresh basil for serving.

Per serving:

Calories: 402; fat: 5g; carbs: 24g; protein: 65g

Shredded Chicken Souvlaki

Ingredients: *(Time: 6-8 hours 10 minutes)*

- 3 pounds boneless, skinless chicken thighs
- ⅓ cup water

- ⅓ cup freshly squeezed lemon juice
- ¼ cup red wine vinegar
- 4 garlic cloves, minced
- 2 tablespoons extra-virgin olive oil
- 2 teaspoons dried oregano
- ¼ teaspoon sea salt
- ¼ teaspoon freshly ground black pepper

Method: (Servings: 6).

1. In a slow cooker, combine the chicken, water, lemon juice, vinegar, garlic, olive oil, oregano, salt, and pepper. Stir to mix well.
2. Cover the cooker and cook for 6 to 8 hours on Low heat.
3. Transfer the chicken from the slow cooker to a work surface.
4. Using 2 forks, shred the chicken, return it to the slow cooker, mix it with the sauce, and keep it warm until ready to serve.

Per serving:

Calories: 462; fat: 28g; carbs: 3g; protein: 48g

Chicken Caprese Casserole

Ingredients: (Time: 6-8 hours 10 minutes)

- 2 pounds boneless, skinless chicken thighs, cut into 1-inch cubes
- 1 (15-ounce) can no-salt-added diced tomatoes
- 2 cups fresh basil leaves (about 1 large bunch)
- ¼ cup extra-virgin olive oil
- 2½ tablespoons balsamic vinegar
- ½ teaspoon sea salt
- ⅛ teaspoon freshly ground black pepper
- 2 cups shredded mozzarella cheese

Method: (Servings: 4).

1. In a slow cooker, layer the chicken, tomatoes, and basil. In a small bowl, whisk together the olive oil, vinegar, salt, and pepper until blended.
2. Pour the dressing into the slow cooker. Stir to mix well.
3. Cover the cooker and cook for 6 to 8 hours on Low heat.
4. Sprinkle the mozzarella cheese on top. Replace the cover on the cooker and cook for 10 to 20 minutes on Low heat, or until the cheese melts.
5. Enjoy this chicken caprese casserole as is or serve it over cooked pasta or rice.

Per serving:

Calories: 569; fat: 40g; carbs: 9g; protein: 47g

Rosemary Chicken with Potatoes

Ingredients: (Time: 6-8 hours 20 minutes)

- 1 tablespoon olive oil
- 2 pounds boneless, skinless chicken thighs
- 1/2 teaspoon kosher salt
- 1/2 teaspoon freshly ground black pepper
- 6 small red potatoes, halved
- 1 leek (white and pale green parts only), sliced into 1" pieces
- 6 sprigs rosemary, divided
- 1 garlic clove, minced
- 1/2 cup Roasted Chicken Broth
- 1/4 cup capers

Method: (Servings: 6).

1. Heat the olive oil in a large skillet over medium heat until hot but not smoking.
2. Add chicken, and season with salt and pepper. Cook for 5 minutes on one side and flip.

3. Cook for an additional 5 minutes. Place the potatoes and leek into a 4- to 5-quart slow cooker.

4. Top with 5 sprigs of rosemary and garlic. Place chicken thighs on the rosemary.

5. Pour broth over chicken and potatoes. Cover and cook on high for 3 –4 hours or until the juices run clear from the chicken.

6. Sprinkle with capers just before serving, and garnish with remaining rosemary.

Per serving:

Calories: 336, fat: 9g, carbs: 30g, protein: 33g

Mediterranean Roasted Turkey Breast

Ingredients: (Time: 6-8 hours 15 minutes)

- 3 garlic cloves, minced
- 1 teaspoon sea salt
- 1 teaspoon dried oregano
- ½ teaspoon freshly ground black pepper
- ½ teaspoon dried basil
- ½ teaspoon dried parsley
- ½ teaspoon dried rosemary
- ½ teaspoon dried thyme
- ¼ teaspoon dried dill
- ¼ teaspoon ground nutmeg
- 2 tablespoons extra-virgin olive oil
- 2 tablespoons freshly squeezed lemon juice
- 1 (4- to 6-pound) boneless or bone-in turkey breast
- 1 onion, chopped
- ½ cup low-sodium chicken broth
- 4 ounces whole Kalamata olives, pitted
- 1 cup sun-dried tomatoes (packaged, not packed in oil), chopped

Method: (Servings: 4).

1. In a small bowl, stir together the garlic, salt, oregano, pepper, basil, parsley, rosemary, thyme, dill, and nutmeg.
2. Drizzle the olive oil and lemon juice all over the turkey breast and generously season it with the garlic-spice mix.
3. In a slow cooker, combine the onion and chicken broth. Place the seasoned turkey breast on top of the onion. Top the turkey with the olives and sun-dried tomatoes.
4. Cover the cooker and cook for 6 to 8 hours on Low heat. 5.Slice or shred the turkey for serving.

Per serving:

Calories: 761; fat: 55g; carbs: 20g; protein: 83g

Chicken Pesto Polenta

Ingredients: (Time: 4-6 hours 10 minutes)

- 4 (4-ounce) boneless, skinless chicken breasts, cut into bite-sized pieces
- 1 cup prepared pesto, divided
- 1 medium onion, peeled and finely diced
- 4 cloves garlic, minced
- 1 1/2 teaspoons dried Italian seasoning
- 1 (16-ounce) tube prepared polenta, cut into 1/2" slices
- 2 cups chopped fresh spinach
- 1 (14 1/2-ounce) can diced tomatoes
- 1 (8-ounce) bag shredded low-fat Italian cheese blend

Method: (Servings: 6).

1. In a large bowl, combine chicken pieces with pesto, onion, garlic, and Italian seasoning.

2. In a greased 4- to 5-quart slow cooker, layer half of chicken mixture, half the polenta, half the spinach, and half the tomatoes.
3. Continue to layer, ending with tomatoes. Cover and cook on low for 4 –6 hours or on high for 2–3 hours. Top with cheese.

4. Cover and continue to cook for 45 minutes to an hour until cheese has melted.

Per serving:

Calories: 535, fat: 16g, carbs: 65g, protein: 32g

Turkey Piccata

Ingredients: (Time: 5-7 hours 10 minutes)

- 1½ pounds new potatoes, halved
- 2 pounds boneless, skinless turkey breast fillets or thighs
- 1 cup low-sodium chicken broth
- Juice of 2 lemons
- 1 tablespoon extra-virgin olive oil
- ¼ cup drained capers
- 1 teaspoon sea salt
- 1 teaspoon dried parsley
- ¼ teaspoon freshly ground black pepper
- 1 tablespoon unsalted butter, melted
- 2 tablespoons chopped fresh parsley

Method: (Servings: 4).

1. Put the potatoes in a slow cooker and place the turkey on top of the potatoes.
2. In a small bowl, whisk together the chicken broth, lemon juice, olive oil, capers, salt, parsley, pepper, and melted butter until combined. Pour this sauce over the turkey.
3. Cover the cooker and cook for 5 to 7 hours on Low heat.

4. Garnish with fresh parsley for serving.

Per serving:

Calories: 427; fat: 8g; carbs: 30g; protein: 60g

Chicken Piccata

Ingredients: (Time: 2-3 hours 10 minutes)

- 2 large (6-ounce) boneless, skinless chicken breasts, cut horizontally into very thin slices
- 1 cup all-purpose flour
- 1 tablespoon olive oil
- 1/4 cup lemon juice
- 3 tablespoons nonpareil capers
- 3/4 cup chicken stock
- 1/4 teaspoon freshly ground black pepper

Method: (Servings: 4).

1. Dredge both sides of the chicken breast slices in the flour. Discard leftover flour. Heat olive oil in a non-stick pan over medium-high heat.
2. Quickly sear the chicken on both sides to brown, approximately 1 minute per side.
3. Place the chicken, lemon juice, capers, stock, and pepper into a greased 4- to 5-quart slow cooker.
4. Cook on high for 2–3 hours or on low for 4 –6 hours until the chicken is cooked through and the sauce has thickened.

Per serving:

Calories: 260, fat: 6.5g, protein: 22g, carbs: 27g

Pesto Chicken and Potatoes

Ingredients: (Time: 4-6 hours 15 minutes)

For The Pesto

- 1 cup fresh basil leaves
- 1 garlic clove, crushed
- ¼ cup pine nuts
- ¼ cup grated Parmesan cheese
- 2 tablespoons extra-virgin olive oil, plus more as needed
- 1 teaspoon sea salt
- ½ teaspoon freshly ground black pepper

For The Chicken

- Non-stick cooking spray
- 2 pounds red potatoes, quartered
- 3 pounds boneless, skinless chicken thighs
- ½ cup low-sodium chicken broth

Method: (Servings: 4).

1. In a food processor, combine the basil, garlic, pine nuts, Parmesan cheese, olive oil, salt, and pepper.
2. Pulse until smooth, adding more olive oil ½ teaspoon at a time if needed until any clumps are gone. Set aside.
3. Coat a slow-cooker insert with cooking spray and put the potatoes into the prepared slow cooker.
4. Place the chicken on top of the potatoes.
5. In a medium bowl, whisk together the pesto and broth until combined and pour the mixture over the chicken.
6. Cover the cooker and cook for 6 to 8 hours on Low heat.

Per serving:

166

Calories: 467; fat: 24g; carbs: 25g; protein: 38g

Turkey Kofta Casserole

Ingredients: *(Time: 6-8 hours 20 minutes)*

For The Kofta

- 2 pounds' raw ground turkey
- 1 small onion, diced
- 3 garlic cloves, minced
- 2 tablespoons chopped fresh parsley
- 1 tablespoon ground coriander
- 2 teaspoons ground cumin
- 1 teaspoon sea salt
- 1 teaspoon freshly ground black pepper
- ½ teaspoon ground nutmeg
- ½ teaspoon dried mint
- ½ teaspoon paprika

For The Casserole

- Non-stick cooking spray
- 2½ pounds potatoes, peeled and cut into ¼-inch-thick rounds
- 3 pounds' tomatoes, cut into ¼-inch-thick rounds
- Salt
- Freshly ground black pepper
- 8-ounce can no-salt-added, no-sugar-added tomato sauce

Method: *(Servings: 4).*

1. In a large bowl, mix together the turkey, onion, garlic, parsley, coriander, cumin, salt, pepper, nutmeg, mint, and paprika until combined.

2. Form the kofta mixture into 13 to 15 equal patties, using about 2 to 3 tablespoons of the meat mixture per patty.
3. Coat a slow-cooker insert with cooking spray.
4. Layer the kofta patties, potatoes, and tomatoes in the prepared slow cooker, alternating the ingredients as you go, like a ratatouille. Season with salt and pepper.
5. Spread the tomato sauce over the ingredients.
6. Cover the cooker and cook for 6 to 8 hours on Low heat, or until the potatoes are tender.

Per serving:

Calories: 588; fat: 17g; carbs: 61g; protein: 52g

Lemon Garlic Chicken

Ingredients: (Time: 6-8 hours 10 minutes)

- 3 pounds boneless, skinless chicken thighs
- ½ cup low-sodium chicken broth ¼ cup freshly squeezed lemon juice
- 4 garlic cloves, minced
- 1 teaspoon grated lemon zest
- 1 teaspoon extra-virgin olive oil
- 1 teaspoon sea salt
- ½ teaspoon freshly ground black pepper
- ½ teaspoon dried thyme, parsley, or basil (or other herb of your choice)

Method: (Servings: 6).

1. In a slow cooker, combine the chicken, chicken broth, lemon juice, garlic, lemon zest, olive oil, salt, pepper, and your preferred herb. Stir to mix well.
2. Cover the cooker and cook for 6 to 8 hours on Low heat.

Per serving:

Calories: 187; fat: 10g; carbs: 2g; protein: 22g

Chicken with Olives and Capers

Ingredients: *(Time: 6-8 hours 10 minutes)*

- 2 pounds bone-in, skin-on chicken thighs or legs
- 1 (5¾-ounce) jar green olives, with juice
- 1 (3½-ounce) jar capers, with juice
- 2 tablespoons red wine vinegar
- 1 garlic clove, minced
- 1 teaspoon dried oregano
- ¼ teaspoon sea salt
- ⅛ teaspoon freshly ground black pepper
- 2 tablespoons chopped fresh basil

Method: *(Servings: 4).*

1. Put the chicken in a slow cooker and top it with the olives and their juice and the capers and their juice.
2. Pour the vinegar over the chicken and sprinkle the garlic, oregano, salt, and pepper on top.
3. Cover the cooker and cook for 6 to 8 hours on Low heat.
4. Garnish with fresh basil for serving.

Per serving:

Calories: 553; fat: 40g; Carbs: 1g; Protein: 39g

Rosemary Chicken and Potatoes

Ingredients: *(Time: 6-8 hours 10 minutes)*

- 2 pounds red potatoes, quartered
- 2½ pounds bone-in, skin-on chicken thighs
- ¼ cup low-sodium chicken broth
- 2 tablespoons dried rosemary
- 1 teaspoon sea salt
- ½ teaspoon freshly ground black pepper
- 2 tablespoons extra-virgin olive oil

Method: (Servings: 4).

1. Put the potatoes in a slow cooker and arrange the chicken on top. Pour the chicken broth over the chicken and potatoes.
2. Sprinkle the rosemary, salt, and pepper on top of the chicken and potatoes, and drizzle the chicken with the olive oil.
3. Cover the cooker and cook for 6 to 8 hours on Low heat.

Per serving:

Calories: 833; fat: 51g; carbs: 37g; protein: 53g

Greek Chicken Kebabs

Ingredients: (Time: 6-8 hours 20 minutes)

- 2 pounds boneless, skinless chicken thighs, cut into 1-inch cubes
- 2 zucchini (nearly 1 pound), cut into 1-inch pieces
- 1 green bell pepper, seeded and cut into 1-inch pieces
- 1 red bell pepper, seeded and cut into 1-inch pieces
- 1 large red onion, chopped
- 2 tablespoons extra-virgin olive oil
- 2 tablespoons freshly squeezed lemon juice
- 1 tablespoon red wine vinegar
- 2 garlic cloves, minced

- 1 teaspoon sea salt
- 1 teaspoon dried oregano
- ½ teaspoon dried basil
- ½ teaspoon dried thyme
- ¼ teaspoon freshly ground black pepper

Method: *(Servings: 4).*

1. In a slow cooker, combine the chicken, zucchini, green and red bell peppers, onion, olive oil, lemon juice, vinegar, garlic, salt, oregano, basil, thyme, and black pepper. Stir to mix well.
2. Cover the cooker and cook for 6 to 8 hours on Low heat.
3. Serve with this tzatziki sauce

Per serving:

Calories: 375; fat: 21g; carbs: 13g; protein: 34g

Chicken with Dates and Almonds

Ingredients: *(Time: 4-6 hours 15 minutes)*

- 1 (15-ounce) can reduced-sodium chickpeas, drained and rinsed
- 2½ pounds bone-in, skin-on chicken thighs
- ½ cup low-sodium chicken broth
- 2 garlic cloves, minced
- 1 teaspoon sea salt
- 1 teaspoon ground cumin
- ½ teaspoon ground ginger
- ½ teaspoon ground coriander
- ¼ teaspoon ground cinnamon
- ¼ teaspoon freshly ground black pepper
- ½ cup dried dates ¼ cup sliced almonds

***Method:** (Servings: 4).*

1. In a slow cooker, gently toss together the onion and chickpeas.
2. Place the chicken on top of the chickpea mixture and pour the chicken broth over the chicken.
3. In a small bowl, stir together the garlic, salt, cumin, ginger, coriander, cinnamon, and pepper. Sprinkle the spice mix over everything.
4. Top with the dates and almonds.
5. Cover the cooker and cook for 6 to 8 hours on Low heat.

Per serving:

Calories: 841; fat: 48g; carbs: 41g; protein: 57g

Meat

Mediterranean Pork Souvlaki

Ingredients: *(Time: 4 hours 15 minutes)*

- 2 pounds' pork shoulder, cubed
- 1 red bell pepper, sliced
- 1 yellow bell pepper, sliced
- 1 red onion, sliced
- 4 cloves garlic, minced
- ¼ cup olive oil
- ¼ cup lemon juice
- 2 teaspoons dried oregano
- Salt and pepper to taste
- Wooden skewers, soaked in water

Method: *(Servings: 5).*

1. In a bowl, combine pork, bell peppers, red onion, and garlic.
2. In a separate bowl, whisk together olive oil, lemon juice, oregano, salt, and pepper.
3. Pour the marinade over the pork mixture and toss to coat evenly. Let it marinate for 1 hour.
4. Thread the marinated pork and vegetables onto the soaked skewers.
5. Place skewers in the crock pot and cook on low for 4 hours.
6. Serve with pita bread and tzatziki.

Per serving:

Calories: 599; fat: 43g; carb: 5g; protein: 46g

Beef Stroganoff

Ingredients: *(Time: 8 hours 15 minutes)*

- 2 pounds' beef stew meat, cubed
- 1 onion, finely chopped
- 8 oz. mushrooms, sliced
- 3 cloves garlic, minced
- 1 cup beef broth
- ½ cup dry red wine
- 2 tablespoons tomato paste
- 1 teaspoon dried thyme
- 1 teaspoon paprika
- 1 cup sour cream
- Salt and pepper to taste
- Fresh parsley for garnish

Method: *(Servings: 6).*

1. In a crock pot, combine beef, onion, mushrooms, and garlic.
2. In a bowl, mix beef broth, red wine, tomato paste, thyme, paprika, salt, and pepper. Pour over the beef mixture.
3. Cover and cook on low for 8 hours.
4. Stir in sour cream just before serving.
5. Garnish with fresh parsley and serve over egg noodles or rice.

Per serving:

Calories: 325; fat: 17g; carb: 41g; protein: 6g

Lamb and Chickpea Tagine

Ingredients: *(Time: 6 hours 20 minutes)*

- 2 pounds' lamb shoulder, cubed
- 1 can (15 oz) chickpeas, drained and rinsed
- 2 large carrots, sliced
- 1 onion, chopped
- 3 cloves garlic, minced
- 1 teaspoon ground cumin
- 1 teaspoon ground coriander
- 1 teaspoon ground cinnamon
- 1 cup chicken broth
- ½ cup dried apricots, chopped
- Salt and pepper to taste
- Fresh cilantro for garnish

Method: (Servings: 4).

1. Brown lamb in a skillet over medium-high heat; transfer to the crock pot.
2. Add chickpeas, carrots, onion, and garlic to the crock pot.
3. In a bowl, mix cumin, coriander, cinnamon, salt, and pepper. Sprinkle over the lamb and vegetables.
4. Pour in chicken broth and add dried apricots.
5. Cover and cook on low for 6 hours. Garnish with fresh cilantro before serving.

Per serving:

Calories: 475; fat: 20g; carb: 24g; protein: 51g

Pork and Olive Ragout

Ingredients: (Time: 7 hours 15 minutes)

- 2 pounds' pork loin, cubed
- 1 cup Kalamata olives, pitted
- 1 can (14 oz.) diced tomatoes

- 1 onion, finely chopped
- 4 cloves garlic, minced
- ½ cup dry white wine
- 2 tablespoons capers
- 1 teaspoon dried rosemary
- 1 teaspoon dried thyme
- Salt and pepper to taste

Method: *(Servings: 6).*

1. In the crock pot, combine pork, olives, diced tomatoes, onion, and garlic.
2. Pour in white wine and add capers, rosemary, thyme, salt, and pepper.
3. Stir well and cook on low for 7 hours.
4. Adjust seasoning if needed and serve over couscous or mashed potatoes.

Per serving:

Calories: 387; fat: 21g; carb: 6g; protein: 42g

Greek-Style Slow Cooked Beef Gyros

Ingredients: *(Time: 6 hours 15 minutes)*

- 2 pounds' beef sirloin, thinly sliced
- 1 large red onion, thinly sliced
- 1 cup cherry tomatoes, halved
- 4 cloves garlic, minced
- ¼ cup olive oil
- ¼ cup red wine vinegar
- 1 tablespoon dried oregano
- 1 teaspoon ground cumin
- 1 teaspoon smoked paprika
- Salt and pepper to taste

- Pita bread and Tzatziki for serving

Method: (Servings: 5).

1. In a bowl, combine beef, red onion, cherry tomatoes, and garlic.
2. In a separate bowl, whisk together olive oil, red wine vinegar, oregano, cumin, paprika, salt, and pepper.
3. Pour the marinade over the beef mixture and toss to coat evenly. Let it marinate for 1 hour.
4. Transfer the marinated mixture to the crock pot.
5. Cover and cook on low for 6 hours. Stir occasionally. Serve the beef gyro mixture in warm pita bread with a generous dollop of Tzatziki.

Per serving:

Calories: 576; fat: 30g; carb: 9g; protein: 44g

Mediterranean Beef and Rice

Ingredients: (Time: 8 hours 10 minutes)

- 1 ½ tablespoons Garam Masala Spice
- 1 tablespoon Beef Bouillon Granules
- 1 teaspoon Mediterranean Spiced Sea Salt
- 1 teaspoon Seasoned Salt
- ½ teaspoon Ground Turmeric
- ½ teaspoon Freshly Ground Black Pepper
- ½ teaspoon Ground Cinnamon
- ½ teaspoon Ground Ginger
- 3 pounds Beef Pot Roast (cut into small pieces, or use beef stew meat)
- 16 ounces Frozen Mixed Vegetables (or substitute fresh vegetables)
- 3 cloves Garlic (minced)
- 2 cups Water

- 1 cup Pine Nuts (toasted)
- 2 cups Rice (for serving)

Method: *(Servings: 12).*

1. In a small mixing bowl, combine together the garam masala, beef bouillon granules, sea salt, season all, turmeric, black pepper, cinnamon and ginger.
2. Toss meat with spices.
3. Add seasoned meat, water, vegetables and minced garlic to a 6 quart or larger slow cooker.
4. Cover and cook on low for 8 hours.
5. Before serving, mix in toasted pine nuts Serve over rice.

Per serving:

Calories: 337; fat: 20g; carb: 17g; protein: 30g

Pineapple-Pork Tacos

Ingredients: *(Time: 7 hours 20 minutes)*

- 1 lb boneless pork shoulder roast, trimmed
- 1 package (1 oz.) taco seasoning mix
- 1 can (8 oz.) pineapple tidbits in juice, drained
- 2 teaspoons lime juice
- 1 box (4.6 oz.) Crunchy Taco Shells
- ¾ cup shredded Cheddar cheese (3 oz.)
- 1 ½ cups shredded lettuce
- ¾ cup chopped tomato
- 1/3 cup sour cream
- 1/3 cup salsa

Method: *(Servings: 6).*

1. Spray a slow cooker with cooking spray. Place pork in slow cooker; sprinkle with taco seasoning mix.
2. Cover; cook on Low heat setting 7 to 9 hours or until pork pulls apart easily with fork.
3. Remove pork from slow cooker; shred pork. Stir into liquid in slow cooker. Stir in pineapple and lime juice.
4. To serve, divide pork among taco shells (about 1/4 cup each), and top with remaining ingredients.

Per serving:

Calories: 200; fat: 6g; carb: 15g; protein: 20g

Beef and Spinach Lasagna

Ingredients: (Time: 4-6 hours 30 minutes)

- 1 pound ground beef
- 1 onion, chopped
- 2 cloves garlic, minced
- 1 can (28 ounces) crushed tomatoes
- 1 can (6 ounces) tomato paste
- 1 teaspoon dried basil
- 1 teaspoon dried oregano
- Salt and black pepper to taste
- 8 lasagna noodles, cooked and drained
- 1 ½ cups ricotta cheese
- 2 cups shredded mozzarella cheese
- 2 cups fresh spinach leaves
- Grated Parmesan cheese for topping
- Fresh basil leaves for garnish (optional)

Method: (Servings: 6).

1. In a skillet, brown the ground beef with chopped onion and minced garlic.
2. Drain any excess fat. 2.Stir in crushed tomatoes, tomato paste, dried basil, dried oregano, salt, and black pepper.
3. In the crock pot, layer some of the meat sauce, followed by a layer of cooked lasagna noodles, a layer of ricotta cheese, a layer of shredded mozzarella cheese, and a layer of fresh spinach leaves. Repeat the layers.
4. Top with a final layer of meat sauce and sprinkle with grated Parmesan cheese.
5. Cover and cook on low for 4-6 hours or until the lasagna is hot and bubbly. 6.Serve hot, garnished with fresh basil leaves if desired.

Per serving:

Calories: 3922; fat: 13g; carb: 44g; protein: 23g

Lamb and Bean Stew

Ingredients: (Time: 3 hours 15 minutes)

- ½ lb of lamb stew meat
- 1 lb pre-soaked pinto beans
- 8-10 medium red potatoes
- 4 medium carrots
- 2 large Spanish onions
- 1 celery heart
- 1 large zucchini
- ¾ cup soy sauce garlic powder

Method: (Servings: 6).

1. After spraying your slow cooker with oil add diced onions, sliced carrots and celery.
2. Add your beans. If you are running short on time, or do not have pre-soaked beans, you can use low sodium white beans.

3. Add Lamb stew meat.
4. Top with diced zucchini and red potatoes.
5. Cover with soy sauce and water. Cook for 3 hours on high. Serve hot!

Per serving:

Calories: 681; fat: 11g; carb: 124g; protein: 25g

Teriyaki Beef and Broccoli

Ingredients: *(Time: 6 hours 20 minutes)*

- 2 cups beef broth
- ½ cup low-sodium soy sauce
- ⅓ cup packed brown sugar
- 1 ½ teaspoon sesame oil
- 1 clove garlic minced
- 1 ½ lb beef top sirloin steak sliced into ½ inch thick strips
- 2 tablespoon corn starch
- ¼ cup cold water
- 4 cups broccoli florets steamed

Method: *(Servings: 4).*

1. Combine the first 5 ingredients in a slow cooker. Add beef and stir to coat. Cover.
2. Set slow cooker on low and cook until tender. 6 hours on low or 4 hours on high.
3. In a small bowl whisk together corn-starch and water until smooth. Add to hot liquid in slow cooker and stir.
4. Cover and cook until teriyaki sauce has thickened, about 30 minutes. 6.Serve over hot rice and topped with steamed broccoli.
5. Garnish with sliced green onions and sesame seeds if desired.

Per serving:

Calories: 498; fat: 21g; carb: 35g; protein: 41g

Pork and Sweet Corn Chowder

Ingredients: *(Time: 6-8 hours 15 minutes)*

- 2 pounds' pork baby back ribs
- 1 cup blackberry jam
- ½ cup BBQ sauce
- ¼ cup apple cider vinegar
- 2 cloves garlic, minced
- Salt and black pepper to taste

Method: *(Servings: 4).*

1. Season the pork baby back ribs with salt and black pepper.
2. Place the ribs in the crock pot.
3. In a bowl, mix blackberry jam, BBQ sauce, apple cider vinegar, and minced garlic.
4. Pour the sauce mixture over the ribs in the crock pot.
5. Cover and cook on low for 6-8 hours or until the ribs are tender and cooked through. Serve hot.

Per serving:

Calories: 583; fat: 36g; carb: 21g; protein: 46g

Slow Cooker Beef Curry

Ingredients: *(Time: 8 hours 15 minutes)*

- 1 (14.5 ounce) can diced tomatoes, undrained
- 1 large onion, sliced
- 1 cup beef broth

- 1 cup coconut milk
- 3 tablespoons curry powder
- 3 cloves garlic, pressed
- 2 bay leaves
- 1 teaspoon minced fresh ginger root
- 1 teaspoon cayenne pepper, or more to taste (Optional)
- 1 whole star anise
- Salt and ground black pepper to taste
- 1 (1 ½-pound) flank steak
- ½ lime, juiced

Method: *(Servings: 6).*

1. Combine diced tomatoes with their juices, onion, beef broth, coconut milk, curry powder, garlic, bay leaves, ginger, cayenne pepper, star anise, salt, and pepper in the bottom of a slow cooker.
2. Stir to combine. Add flank steak to the mixture.
3. Cover and cook on Low until beef are tender and cooked through, about 8 hours.
4. Add lime juice just prior to serving.

Per serving:

Calories: 181; fat: 12g; carb: 13g; protein: 9g

Pork and Pumpkin Chili

Ingredients: *(Time: 6-8 hours 20 minutes)*

- 2 pounds ground pork
- 1 onion, chopped
- 2 cloves garlic, minced
- 1 can (14 ounces) diced tomatoes
- 1 can (14 ounces) pumpkin puree

- 2 cans (15 ounces each) black beans, drained and rinsed
- 1 can (4 ounces) diced green chilies
- 2 tablespoons chili powder
- 1 teaspoon ground cumin
- ½ teaspoon ground cinnamon
- ½ teaspoon ground nutmeg
- Salt and black pepper to taste

For garnish (optional)

- Shredded cheddar cheese, chopped
- Green onions
- Sour cream

Method: (Servings: 6).

1. In a skillet, brown the ground pork over medium-high heat, breaking it into crumbles. Drain any excess fat.
2. Transfer the cooked pork to the crock pot.
3. Add chopped onions, minced garlic, diced tomatoes, pumpkin puree, black beans, diced green chilies, chili powder, cumin, ground cinnamon, ground nutmeg, salt, and black pepper.
4. Stir to combine all ingredients.
5. Cover and cook on low for 6-8 hours. Serve hot, garnished with shredded cheddar cheese, chopped green onions, and sour cream if desired.

Per serving:

Calories: 1053; fat: 66g; carb: 50g; protein: 73g

Lamb Chili with Lentils

Ingredients: (Time: 6-8 hours 10 minutes)

- 1 tablespoon extra-virgin olive oil
- 2 pounds' raw ground lamb
- 1 (28-ounce) can no-salt-added crushed tomatoes
- 2½ cups water
- 1 onion, finely chopped
- 1 green bell pepper, seeded and diced
- ¾ cup dried lentils, any color
- 2 garlic cloves, minced
- 1 tablespoon chili powder
- 1 tablespoon ground cumin
- 1½ teaspoons sea salt
- 1 teaspoon dried oregano
- ½ teaspoon freshly ground black pepper

Method: (Servings: 4).

1. Heat the olive oil in a large skillet over medium-high heat.
2. Add the ground lamb and cook for 3 to 5 minutes, breaking up the meat with a spoon, until it has browned and is no longer pink. Drain any grease and transfer the lamb to a slow cooker.
3. Add the tomatoes, water, onion, bell pepper, lentils, garlic, chili powder, cumin, salt, oregano, and black pepper to the lamb. Stir to mix well.
4. Cover the cooker and cook for 6 to 8 hours on Low heat, or until the lentils are tender.
5. Top this chili with your favorite Mediterranean garnishes, such as crumbled feta cheese and fresh herbs like chopped chives or parsley.

Per serving:

Calories: 540; fat: 32g; carbs: 36g; protein: 31g

Rosemary Leg of Lamb

Ingredients: *(Time: 8-10 hours 10 minutes)*

- 2 cups low-sodium beef broth
- 2 rosemary sprigs (optional)
- 1 (3- to 4-pound) bone-in lamb leg
- 1 tablespoon extra-virgin olive oil
- 3 large garlic cloves, minced
- 1½ teaspoons dried rosemary
- 1 teaspoon sea salt
- ½ teaspoon freshly ground black pepper

Method: *(Servings: 6-8).*

1. In a slow cooker, combine the beef broth and rosemary sprigs (if using).
2. Rub the lamb all over with olive oil and season it with garlic, rosemary, salt, and pepper. Add the lamb to the slow cooker.
3. Cover the cooker and cook for 8 to 10 hours on Low heat, or until the lamb is tender.
4. You can make a nice gravy out of the drippings from the slow cooker:
5. Once the lamb is cooked, strain the juices into a small saucepan and place it over medium-high heat.
6. In a small bowl, whisk together ¼ cup of all-purpose flour and ½ cup of water until smooth to make a slurry. Whisk the slurry into the cooking juices. Bring the mixture to a boil.
7. Cook, stirring constantly, for 1 to 2 minutes until thickened.

Per serving:

Calories: 353; fat: 16g; carbs: 1g; protein: 48g

Braised Lamb Shanks

Ingredients: *(Time: 8 -10 hours 10 minutes)*

- 1 onion, diced

- 1 (28-ounce) no-salt-added, whole peeled tomatoes, with juice
- 2 large carrots, diced
- 3 garlic cloves, minced
- 1 cup low-sodium beef broth
- 1 teaspoon sea salt
- 1 teaspoon dried rosemary
- 1 teaspoon dried thyme
- 4 lamb shanks (about 3 pounds)

Method: *(Servings: 4).*

1. In a slow cooker, combine the onion, tomatoes and their juice, carrots, garlic, beef broth, salt, rosemary, and thyme. Stir to mix well.
2. Nestle the lamb shanks into the tomato mixture.
3. Cover the cooker and cook for 8 to 10 hours on Low heat.

Per serving:

Calories: 527; fat: 18g; carbs: 16g; protein: 73g

Beef Meatballs in Garlic Cream Sauce

Ingredients: *(Time: 6-8 hours 45 minutes)*

For The Sauce

- 1 cup low-sodium vegetable broth or low-sodium chicken broth
- 1 tablespoon extra-virgin olive oil 2 garlic cloves, minced

- 1 tablespoon dried onion flakes 1 teaspoon dried rosemary
- 2 tablespoons freshly squeezed lemon juice

- Pinch sea salt
- Pinch freshly ground black pepper

For The Meatballs

- 1-pound raw ground beef
- 1 large egg
- 2 tablespoons bread crumbs
- 1 teaspoon ground cumin
- 1 teaspoon salt
- ½ teaspoon freshly ground black pepper

To Finish

- 2 cups plain Greek yogurt
- 2 tablespoons chopped fresh parsley

Method: *(Servings: 6-8).*

1. In a medium bowl, whisk together the vegetable broth, olive oil, garlic, onion flakes, rosemary, lemon juice, salt, and pepper until combined.
2. In a large bowl, mix together the ground beef, egg, bread crumbs, cumin, salt, and pepper until combined. Shape the meat mixture into 10 to 12 (2½-inch) meatballs.
3. Pour the sauce into the slow cooker.
4. Add the meatballs to the slow cooker. 3.Cover the cooker and cook for 6 to 8 hours on Low heat.
5. Stir in the yogurt. Replace the cover on the cooker and cook for 15 to 30 minutes on Low heat, or until the sauce has thickened.
6. Garnish with fresh parsley for serving.

Per serving:

Calories: 345; fat: 20g; carbohydrates: 13g; protein: 29g

Italian Short Rib Stew

Ingredients: *(Time: 6-8 hours 15 minutes)*

- 3 pounds' boneless beef short ribs, cut into 1-inch pieces
- 1½ pounds red potatoes, quartered
- 4 carrots, cut into ½-inch cubes
- 4 ounces mushrooms, sliced
- 1 large onion, diced
- 1 (28-ounce) can no-salt-added diced tomatoes
- 1 cup low-sodium beef broth
- 2 garlic cloves, minced
- 1 tablespoon dried thyme
- 1½ teaspoons dried parsley
- 1½ teaspoons sea salt
- ½ teaspoon freshly ground black pepper

Method: *(Servings: 6).*

1. In a slow cooker, combine the short ribs, potatoes, carrots, mushrooms, onion, tomatoes, beef broth, garlic, thyme, parsley, salt, and pepper. Stir to mix well.
2. Cover the cooker and cook for 6 to 8 hours on Low heat.

Per serving:

Calories: 818; fat: 37g; carbs: 49g; protein: 74g

Osso Buco

Ingredients: *(Time: 8-10 hours 10 minutes)*

- 1 (15-ounce) can no-salt-added diced tomatoes
- 1 cup low-sodium beef broth
- 2 carrots, diced 1 small onion, diced 1 celery stalk, diced

- 2 garlic cloves, minced
- 1 teaspoon sea salt
- 2 to 3 pounds' bone-in beef shanks
- 2 tablespoons Italian Seasoning Handful fresh parsley

Method: *(Servings: 4).*

1. In a slow cooker, combine the tomatoes, beef broth, carrots, onion, celery, garlic, and salt. Stir to mix well.
2. Generously season the beef shanks with the Italian seasoning. Nestle the shanks into the vegetable mixture.
3. Cover the cooker and cook for 8 to 10 hours on Low heat.
4. Garnish with fresh parsley for serving.

Per serving:

Calories: 303; fat: 11g; carbs: 22g; protein: 28g

Kofta with Vegetables in Tomato Sauce

Ingredients: *(Time: 6-8 hours 20 minutes)*

- 1-pound raw ground beef
- 1 small white or yellow onion, finely diced
- 2 garlic cloves, minced
- 1 tablespoon dried parsley
- 2 teaspoons ground coriander
- 1 teaspoon ground cumin
- ½ teaspoon sea salt
- ½ teaspoon freshly ground black pepper
- ¼ teaspoon ground nutmeg
- ¼ teaspoon dried mint
- ¼ teaspoon paprika

- 1 (28-ounce) can no-salt-added diced tomatoes
- 2 or 3 zucchini, cut into 1½-inch-thick rounds
- 4 ounces' mushrooms
- 1 large red onion, chopped
- 1 green bell pepper, seeded and chopped

Method: *(Servings: 4).*

1. In large bowl, mix together the ground beef, white or yellow onion, garlic, parsley, coriander, cumin, salt, pepper, nutmeg, mint, and paprika until well combined and all of the spices and onion are well blended into the meat.
2. Form the meat mixture into 10 to 12 oval patties. Set aside.
3. In a slow cooker, combine the tomatoes, zucchini, mushrooms, red onion, and bell pepper. Stir to mix well.
4. Place the kofta patties on top of the tomato mixture.
5. Cover the cooker and cook for 6 to 8 hours on Low heat.

Per serving:

Calories: 263; fat: 9g; carbs: 23g; protein: 27g

Side Dishes & Sauce

Fingerling Potatoes with Herb Vinaigrette

Ingredients: *(Time: 2-4 hours 20 minutes)*

- 2 pounds red or yellow fingerling potatoes, scrubbed
- 1 teaspoon kosher salt
- 1/4 cup lemon juice
- 1/3 cup extra-virgin olive oil
- 1 small shallot, peeled and minced (about 2 tablespoons)
- 1 1/2 teaspoons minced fresh thyme leaves
- 1 tablespoon minced fresh basil leaves
- 1 tablespoon minced fresh oregano leaves
- 1/2 teaspoon Dijon mustard
- 1 teaspoon sugar

Method: *(Servings: 4).*

1. Place potatoes in a medium pot and cover with cold water.
2. Bring to a boil and add the kosher salt to the water.
3. Cook potatoes for 6–8 minutes until fork tender.
4. Drain potatoes and place in a greased 4- to 5-quart slow cooker.
5. In a small bowl, whisk together lemon juice, olive oil, shallot, thyme, basil, oregano, mustard, and sugar.
6. Drizzle vinaigrette over potatoes. Cook on low for 4 hours or on high for 2 hours. Serve warm or cold.

Per serving:

Calories: 326, fat: 18g, carbs: 39g, protein: 4g

Lemon Garlic Green Beans

Ingredients: (Time: 8-10 hours 15 minutes)

- 1 1/2 pounds fresh green beans, trimmed
- 3 tablespoons olive oil
- 3 large shallots, peeled and cut into thin wedges
- 6 cloves garlic, sliced
- 1 tablespoon grated lemon zest
- 1/2 teaspoon kosher salt
- 1/2 teaspoon ground black pepper
- 1/2 cup water

Method: (Servings: 4).

1. Place green beans in a greased 4- to 5-quart slow cooker. Add remaining ingredients over the top of the beans.
2. Cook on low for 8–10 hours.
3. If you like your beans crispier, cook them on high and check after about 3 1/2 hours or on low and check after about 6 hours.
4. Fresh green beans are sturdy enough to withstand very long cooking temperatures without getting mushy.

Per serving:

Calories: 167, fat: 10g, protein: 4g, carbs: 17g

Rosemary Garlic Mashed Potatoes

Ingredients: (Time:3-4 hours 20 minutes)

- 3 pounds medium red potatoes, quartered
- 4 cloves garlic, minced
- 3/4 cup Roasted Chicken Broth

- 1 tablespoon minced fresh rosemary
- 1/4 cup 1% milk 1 tablespoon butter
- 1/3 cup reduced-fat sour cream

Method: (Servings: 10).

1. Place the potatoes in a 4- to 5-quart slow cooker.
2. Add garlic, broth, and rosemary. Stir.
3. Cover and cook on high until potatoes are tender, about 3 -4 hours.
4. Pour in milk, butter, and sour cream. Mash with a potato masher.

Per serving:

Calories: 122, fat: 2g, carbs: 23g, protein: 3.5g

Black Bean Confit

Ingredients: (Time: 8 hours 10 minutes)

- 1 cup dried black beans
- 2 quarts' water
- 1 tablespoon olive oil
- 2 large onions, peeled and diced
- 2 stalks celery, diced
- 2 large carrots, peeled and diced
- 1 clove garlic, diced
- 2 shallots, peeled and thinly sliced
- 1 teaspoon dried thyme
- 1 teaspoon dried oregano
- 1/4 bunch parsley, chopped
- 2 dried or fresh bay leaves
- 1 teaspoon freshly ground black pepper
- 1 (141/2-ounce) can crushed tomatoes

- 1/4 cup Demi-Glace Reduction Sauce
- 1 quart Roasted Chicken Broth

Method: *(Servings: 6).*

1. Soak the beans in the water overnight; rinse and drain them.
2. Grease a 4- to 5-quart slow cooker with oil.
3. Place all of the ingredients in the slow cooker.
4. Cook on low for 8 hours.

Per serving:

Calories: 283, fat: 5g, carbs: 37g, protein: 10g

Prussian Cabbage

Ingredients: *(Time: 2-3 hours 20 minutes)*

- 1 head red cabbage, finely sliced
- 3 apples, cored and sliced
- 4 slices bacon, chopped
- 1/2 cup vinegar
- 2 cups beef broth
- 1/2 teaspoon kosher salt

Method: *(Servings: 6).*

1. Spray a 4- to 5-quart slow cooker with non-stick olive oil spray.
2. Arrange the cabbage, apples, and bacon in the slow cooker.
3. Add the vinegar, beef broth, and salt.
4. Cover and cook on high for 2 –3 hours.

Per serving:

Calories: 154, fat: 7g, carbs: 19g, protein: 5g

Jacques' White Beans

Ingredients: *(Time: 5-8 hours 15 minutes)*

- 2 pounds' white beans 1 ham bone
- 2 cups water 1 bouquet garni
- 1 teaspoon kosher salt
- 3 tablespoons butter
- 3 medium onions, peeled and diced
- 1 clove garlic, sliced
- 1/4 cup chopped parsley
- 1 cup tomato sauce
- 1/2 teaspoon ground black pepper

Method: *(Servings: 10).*

1. In a large bowl, cover beans with cold water.
2. Soak the beans overnight, then drain. Spray a 4- to 5-quart slow cooker with non-stick olive oil spray.
3. Combine beans, ham bone, 2 cups water, bouquet garni, and salt in the slow cooker.
4. Cover and cook on low for 5 –7 hours. Remove the bone and bouquet garni; drain.

5. Heat butter in a large skillet over medium heat. Sauté the onions and garlic until soft.
6. Add the onions, garlic, parsley, tomato sauce, and black pepper to the beans in the slow cooker. Cover and cook for another hour.

Per serving:

Calories: 353, fat: 4g, carbs: 61g, protein: 20g

Spanish Saffron Rice

Ingredients: *(Time: 3-6 hours 20 minutes)*

- 2 tablespoons olive oil
- 1 medium onion, peeled and thinly sliced
- 4 stalks celery, thinly sliced
- 3 medium tomatoes, chopped
- 4 cups water
- 2 teaspoons kosher salt
- 1/4 teaspoon cayenne pepper
- 1 1/3 cups uncooked quinoa
- 1/2 teaspoon saffron threads

Method: *(Servings: 8).*

1. Spray a 4- to 5-quart slow cooker with nonstick olive oil spray.
2. Heat oil in a medium skillet over medium heat. Sauté the onion and celery until soft.
3. Transfer to the slow cooker.
4. Put the tomatoes, water, salt, and cayenne pepper in the slow cooker.
5. Cover and cook on low for 3 –5 hours. Increase heat to high and add quinoa and saffron.

6. Cover slow cooker and allow to cook for 1 hour, or until quinoa is tender.

Per serving:

Calories: 151, fat: 5g, carbs: 21g, protein: 5g

Spicy Fennel and Swiss Chard

Ingredients: *(Time: 2 ½-3 hours 20 minutes)*

- 2 large fennel bulbs, trimmed and chopped

- 1 bundle Swiss chard or kale, trimmed and chopped
- 1/2 cup low-sodium chicken broth
- 2 teaspoons lemon juice
- 1/2 teaspoon kosher salt
- 1/2 teaspoon freshly ground black pepper
- 1/2 teaspoon dried chili flakes

Method: (Servings: 4).

1. Place fennel in a 4- to 5-quart slow cooker and top with Swiss chard or kale.
2. Add remaining ingredients and mi x well. Cover and cook on high for 2 1/2–**3** hours.

Per serving:

Calories: 82, fat: 1g, carbs: 16g, protein: 4g

Cannellini Beans with Pancetta, Rosemary, and Thyme

Ingredients: (Time: 5-8 hours 20 minutes)

- 2 pounds dried cannellini beans
- 2 cups low-sodium chicken broth
- 1/2 teaspoon kosher salt
- 1/2 teaspoon ground white pepper
- 1 tablespoon chopped fresh rosemary
- 1 tablespoon chopped fresh thyme
- 4 slices pancetta, chopped

Method: (Servings: 10).

1. Soak the beans in cold water overnight. Drain and rinse.
2. Place the beans, broth, salt, pepper, rosemary, and thyme in a 4- to 5-quart slow cooker.

3. Cover and cook on low for 6 –8 hours.
4. Place the pancetta in a medium skillet and cook over low heat, stirring occasionally.
5. When the meat is golden brown, after about 5 –8 minutes, drain on paper towels. Serve the beans topped with the crispy pancetta.

Per serving:

Calories: 364, Fat: 5g, Protein: 21g, Carbs: 59g

Herbed Parsnips

Ingredients: *(Time: 4 hours 10 minutes)*

- 2 pounds' parsnips, peeled and chopped
- 2 tablespoons olive oil
- 1/2 teaspoon kosher salt
- 1/2 teaspoon freshly ground black pepper
- 2 teaspoons chopped fresh rosemary
- 2 teaspoons chopped fresh thyme
- 1 teaspoon chopped fresh tarragon
- 1/4 cup chopped flat-leaf parsley

Method: *(Servings: 4).*

1. Place parsnips in a 4- to 5-quart slow cooker and toss with olive oil. Season with salt and pepper.
2. Cover and cook on high for 3 hours. Add rosemary, thyme, and tarragon and cook for 1 more hours.
3. Remove from slow cooker, toss with parsley, and serve.

Per serving:

Calories: 214, Fat: 7g, Carbs: 40g, Protein: 3g

Ghee

Ingredients: *(Time: 2-3 hours 5 minutes)*

- 2 pounds unsalted butter Cut the butter into large cubes.

Method: *(Servings: 36).*

1. Place in a 4- to 5-quart slow cooker.
2. Cover and cook on low for 2 –3 hours. The butter should separate. Don't let it brown.
3. Skim off the clear liquid on the top; this is ghee. Store refrigerated and covered.
4. Discard the butter solids, or use in cooking as a butter substitute.

Per serving:

Calories: 112, fat: 12g, carbs: 0g, protein: 0g

Fresh Tomato Sauce

Ingredients: *(Time: 4-6 hours 20 minutes)*

- 20 large plum tomatoes
- 1 tablespoon olive oil
- 1⁄2 teaspoon kosher salt
- 1⁄2 teaspoon ground red pepper
- 2 large red onions, peeled and diced
- 1 medium shallot, peeled and diced
- 8 cloves garlic, minced
- 1⁄2 teaspoon packed light brown sugar
- 1⁄2 cup dry red wine
- 10 large fresh basil leaves, chopped
- 3 sprigs fresh oregano leaves, chopped

- 1/4 bunch fresh parsley, chopped

Method: *(Servings: 1 gallon).*

1. Bring a large pot of water to a boil. Fill a large bowl with cold water and ice. Gently make a small "x" in the bottom of each tomato, just piercing the skin with a small paring knife.
2. Gently drop the tomatoes into the boiling water using a slotted spoon. Cook for 1 minute.
3. Remove the tomatoes from the boiling water and place them in the ice bath. Let cool and remove the skins. Roughly chop the tomatoes and place in a 4- to 5-quart slow cooker.
4. Heat the oil over medium heat in a saucepan until it shimmers, about 1 minute. Add the salt, red pepper, onions, and shallot and cook until softened, about 5 minutes. Add garlic and brown sugar; cook for 1 minute.
5. Remove from heat and add wine, basil, oregano, and parsley. Transfer mixture to the slow cooker. Stir well.
6. Cook on low for 4 -6 hours. Sauce will keep in the refrigerator for up to 3 days or the freezer for up to 6 months.

Per serving:

Calories: 38, fat: 0.5g, carbs: 6g, protein: 1g

Long-Cooking Traditional Tomato Sauce

Ingredients: *(Time: 6-8 hours 20 minutes)*

- 1 pound sweet Italian sausage, sliced into 1/2" rounds
- 1 tablespoon olive oil
- 2 large onions, peeled and diced
- 2 medium shallots, peeled and diced

- 2 garlic cloves, diced
- 4 (28-ounce) cans plum tomatoes
- 1 cup dry red wine
- 1 cup water
- 1⁄2 teaspoon dried basil
- 1⁄2 teaspoon dried oregano
- 1⁄2 teaspoon dried parsley
- 1⁄2 teaspoon fennel seeds
- 1⁄2 teaspoon kosher salt
- 1⁄2 teaspoon freshly ground black pepper
- 1⁄2 teaspoon red pepper flakes

Method: (Servings: 1 gallon).

1. In a large non-stick skillet over medium heat, cook the sausage until browned, about 5-8 minutes. Remove sausage with a slotted spoon and place in a 6-quart slow cooker.
2. Heat oil over medium heat in a Dutch oven and add onions and shallots. Cook until softened, about 5-8 minutes. Stir in garlic and cook for 1 minute.
3. Add the tomatoes, and cook for 5 minutes. Break tomatoes down with potato masher as they cook.
4. Pour tomato mixture over sausage in the slow cooker. Add remaining ingredients and stir well. Simmer on low heat for 6-8 hours.
5. Serve immediately with pasta, or cool in an ice bath and freeze for up to 3 months.

Per serving:

Calories: 76, fat: 4g, carbs: 5g, protein: 3g

Italian Tomato Sauce with Turkey Meatballs

Ingredients: (Time: 3-6 hours 10 minutes)

- 12 frozen turkey meatballs
- 1 1/2 tablespoons minced fresh basil
- 1 medium onion, peeled and minced
- 1 head roasted garlic (about 2 tablespoons), peels removed
- 1 (28-ounce) can fire-roasted tomatoes
- 1 teaspoon crushed red pepper flakes

Method: *(Servings: 4).*

1. Defrost the meatballs according to package instructions.
2. Place in a 4- to 5-quart slow cooker with the remaining ingredients. Stir.
3. Cook on low for 3–6 hours.
4. Stir before serving.

Per serving:

Calories: 327, fat: 14g, carbs: 21g, protein: 33g

Pink Tomato Sauce

Ingredients: *(Time: 10-12 hours)*

- 1 tablespoon olive oil
- 1 large onion, peeled and diced
- 2 cloves garlic, minced
- 1 tablespoon minced fresh basil
- 1 tablespoon minced fresh Italian parsley
- 2/3 cup fat-free evaporated milk 1 stalk celery, diced
- 1 (15-ounce) can whole tomatoes in purée
- 1 (28-ounce) can crushed tomatoes

Method: *(Servings: 8).*

1. Heat the olive oil in a medium-sized non-stick skillet over medium-high heat.

2. Sauté the onion and garlic until the onion is soft, about 5 minutes.
3. Transfer onion and garlic to a 6-quart slow cooker.
4. Add basil, parsley, evaporated milk, celery, and tomatoes. Stir well.
5. Cook on low for 10–12 hours.

Per serving:

Calories: 80, fat: 3.5g, carbs: 10g, protein: 3g

Tomato and Chicken Sausage Sauce

Ingredients: *(Time: 8 hours 15 minutes)*

- 4 Italian chicken sausages, sliced
- 2 tablespoons tomato paste
- 1 (28-ounce) can crushed tomatoes
- 3 cloves garlic, minced
- 1 medium onion, peeled and minced
- 3 tablespoons minced basil
- 1 tablespoon minced Italian parsley
- 1/4 teaspoon crushed rosemary
- 1/4 teaspoon freshly ground black pepper

Method: *(Servings: 6).*

1. Quickly brown the sausage slices on both sides in a non-stick skillet over medium-high heat.
2. Remove sausages with a slotted spoon and place in a 4- to 5-quart slow cooker, along with the remaining ingredients. Stir.
3. Cook on low for 8 hours.

Per serving:

Calories: 184, fat: 8g, carbs: 8g, protein: 9.5g

Rosemary-Mushroom Sauce

Ingredients: *(Time: 6-8 hours 5 minutes)*

- 1 teaspoon butter
- 1 large onion, peeled and thinly sliced
- 8 ounces sliced mushrooms
- 1 tablespoon crushed rosemary
- 3 cups Roasted Chicken Broth

Method: *(Servings: 4).*

1. Melt the butter in a non-stick skillet over medium heat.
2. Add the onion and mushrooms and sauté until the onion is soft, about 5 minutes.
3. Place the onion and mushrooms into a 4- to 5-quart slow cooker.
4. Add the rosemary and broth. Stir.
5. Cook on low for 6–8 hours or on high for 3 hours.

Per serving:

Calories: 67, fat: 3g, carbs: 14g, protein: 5g

Artichoke Sauce

Ingredients: *(Time: 4 hours)*

- 1 teaspoon olive oil

- 8 ounces frozen artichoke hearts, defrosted
- 3 cloves garlic, minced
- 1 medium onion, peeled and minced
- 2 tablespoons capote capers

- 1 (28-ounce) can crushed tomatoes

Method: (Servings: 4).

1. Heat the oil in a non-stick skillet over medium heat.
2. Sauté the artichokes, garlic, and onion until the onion is translucent and most of the liquid has evaporated, about 8 minutes.
3. Put the mixture into a 4- to 5-quart slow cooker. Stir in the capers and crushed tomatoes.
4. Cook on high for 4 hours or on low for 8 hours.

Per serving:

Calories: 85, fat: 2g, carbs: 16g, protein: 4g

Fennel and Caper Sauce

Ingredients: (Time: 2 hours 35 minutes)

- 2 fennel bulbs with stalks
- 2 tablespoons nonpareil capers
- 1/2 cup Roasted Chicken Broth
- 2 shallots, peeled and thinly sliced
- 2 cups diced fresh tomatoes
- 1/4 teaspoon kosher salt
- 1/2 teaspoon freshly ground black pepper
- 1/3 cup minced fresh parsley

Method: (Servings: 4).

1. Cut off fennel stalks and freeze for soup stock.
2. Reserve 2 tablespoons of the fennel fronds. Thinly slice the fennel bulbs.
3. Place the fennel, capers, broth, shallots, tomatoes, salt, and pepper in a 4- to 5-quart slow cooker. Cook on low for 2 hours, and then add the parsley.
4. Cook an additional 15 –30 minutes on high. Garnish with reserved fronds.

Per serving:

Calories: 76, fat: 0.5g, carbs: 15g, protein: 4g

Regal Caper Sauce

Ingredients: *(Time: 1-2 hours 5 minutes)*

- 2 tablespoons butter
- 2 tablespoons all-purpose flour
- 3 cups chicken stock
- 1/2 teaspoon kosher salt
- 1/2 teaspoon black peppercorns
- 1 large egg yolk
- 1 tablespoon butter
- 6 tablespoons capers

Method: *(Servings: 3).*

1. Spray a 4- to 5-quart slow cooker with non-stick olive oil cooking spray.
2. Melt the butter in a saucepan over medium heat and mix in the flour, stirring until the flour is well mixed and slightly browned.
3. Add the stock and mix well, then transfer to the slow cooker. Add salt and peppercorns.
4. Cover and cook on low for 1 –2 hours.
5. Half an hour before serving, skim with a strainer. Stir in the yolk and butter, then add the capers.

Per serving:

Calories: 114, fat: 8g, carbs: 6g, protein: 4g

Desserts

Apple Pie

Ingredients: (Time: 7 hours 20 minutes)

- 2 pounds of apples
- ¼ cup of granulated sugar
- ¼ cup of breadcrumbs
- 2 tsp of cinnamon, ground
- 3 tbsp. of freshly squeezed lemon juice
- 1 tsp of vanilla sugar
- ¼ cup of oil
- 1 egg, beaten
- ¼ cup of all-purpose flour
- 2 tbsp. of flax seed Pie dough

Method: (Servings: 6).

1. First, peel the apples and cut into bite- sized pieces. Transfer to a large bowl. Add about two to three tablespoons of freshly squeezed lemon juice.
2. Now add breadcrumbs, vanilla sugar, granulated sugar, and cinnamon. You can also add one teaspoon of ground nutmeg in the mixture. Mix well the ingredients and set aside.
3. On a lightly floured surface roll out the pie dough making 2 circle-shaped crusts. Grease the slow cooker with some oil and place one pie crust in it. Spoon the apple mixture and cover with the remaining crust. Seal by crimping edges and brush with beaten egg.
4. I like to sprinkle my pie with flax seed. Also, sprinkle your pie with some nice powdered sugar instead.
5. Cover, set the heat to low and cook for 7 hours.

Per serving:

Calories 214, fat 11g, carbs 27.4g, proteins 2.8g

Classic French Squash Pie

Ingredients: *(Time: 4 hours 15 minutes)*

- 15 oz. mashed squash
- 6 fl oz. whole milk
- ½ tsp of cinnamon, ground
- ½ tsp of nutmeg
- ½ tsp of salt
- 3 large eggs
- ½ cup of granulated sugar
- 1 pack of pate brisee

Method: *(Servings: 8).*

1. Place squash puree in a large bowl.
2. Now add milk, cinnamon, eggs, nutmeg, salt, and sugar. Whisk together until well incorporated.
3. Grease and line the slow cooker with baking paper.
4. Gently place pate brisee creating the edges with your hands. Pour the squash mixture over and flatten the surface with a spatula.
5. Cook on low setting for 4 hours. Turn off the cooker and allow it to stand for 30 minutes.
6. Now gently remove the pie from the cooker and transfer to a serving platter. Refrigerate overnight and serve.

Per serving:

Calories 188, fat 16g, carbs 51g, proteins 7g.

Crème Brûlée

Ingredients: (Time: 2 hours 5 minutes)

- 5 cups of heavy cream
- 8 egg yolks
- 1 cup of sugar plus
- 4 tbsp. for topping
- 1 vanilla bean, split lengthwise
- ¼ tsp of salt

Method: (Servings: 4).

1. In a large bowl, combine heavy cream with egg yolks and sugar. Beat well with an electric mixer on high.
2. Using a sharp knife, scrape the seeds out of your vanilla bean and add them to your heavy cream mixture. Finely chop it and add to the mixture.
3. Now whisk in salt and beat well again. Pour the mixture into four standard-sized ramekins. Set aside.
4. Take 4 x 12" long pieces of aluminum foil and roll them up. Curl each piece into a circle, pinching the ends together. Place in the bottom of your slow cooker.
5. Place each ramekin on aluminum circle and pour enough boiling water to reach up to about 1/3 of the way.
6. Close the cooker's lid and set the heat to low. Cook for two hours, or until the crust is all set.
7. Remove from the slow cooker and add one tablespoon of sugar in each ramekin. Burn evenly with a culinary torch until brown. Chill well and serve.

Per serving:

Calories 226, fat 9g, carbs 19g, proteins 14g

Fig Spread Dessert

Ingredients: *(Time: 2-3 hours 15 minutes)*

- 1 cup of vegetable oil 1 cup of milk
- 1 cup of lukewarm water
- ½ cup of fig spread
- 1 ½ cup of all-purpose flour
- ½ cup of wheat groats
- ½ cup of corn flour
- 2 tsp of baking powder

Topping

- 2 cups of brown sugar
- 2 cups of water
- ½ cup of fig spread

Method: *(Servings: 4).*

1. First, you will have to prepare the topping because it has to chill well before using it. Place sugar, fig spread, and water in a heavy-bottomed pot. Bring it to a boil over medium-high heat and cook for 5 minutes, stirring constantly. Remove from the heat and cool well.
2. In another pot, combine oil with lukewarm water, milk, and the fig spread. Bring it to a boil and then add flour, wheat groats, corn flour, and baking powder. Give it a good stir and mix well continue to cook for 3-4 more minutes. Chill well and form the dough.
3. Using your hands shape 2 inches' thick balls. This mixture should give you about 16 balls, depending on the size you want. Gently flatten the surface and transfer to a lightly greased slow cooker. Cook for 30 minutes on high, then reduce the heat to low and continue to cook for two more hours.
4. Remove from the slow cooker and pour the cold topping over them. Refrigerate for about an hour and serve.

Warm Winter Compote

Ingredients: *(Time: 6-8 hours 20 minutes)*

- 1 lb fresh figs

- 7 oz. Turkish figs
- 7 oz. fresh cherries
- 7 oz. plums
- 3 ½ oz. raisins
- 3 large apples
- 3 tbsp. of corn-starch
- 1 tsp of cinnamon, ground
- 1 tbsp. of cloves
- 1 cup of sugar
- 1 lemon, juiced
- 3 cups of water

Method: *(Servings: 8).*

1. Simply combine the ingredients in a slow cooker and pour 3-4 cups of water (depending on how much liquid you wish.
2. Close the lid and set the heat to low. Cook for 6-8 hours.

Per serving:

Calories 385, fat 1.1g, carbs 100g, proteins 3.1g

Greek Yogurt Berry Parfait

Ingredients: *(Time: 2 hours 15 minutes)*

- 2 cups Greek yogurt
- 1 cup mixed berries (strawberries, blueberries, raspberries)
- ¼ cup honey
- 1 teaspoon vanilla extract
- ½ cup granola

Method: *(Servings: 6).*

1. In a bowl, mix Greek yogurt, honey, and vanilla extract until well combined.
2. Layer the bottom of the crock pot with half of the yogurt mixture.
3. Add half of the mixed berries on top of the yogurt layer.
4. Sprinkle half of the granola evenly over the berries.
5. Repeat the layers with the remaining ingredients.
6. Cover the crock pot and cook on low for 2 hours.
7. Once done, let it cool for 10 minutes before serving.

Per serving:

Calories: 157; fat: 5g; carb: 24g; protein: 4g

Orange and Almond Rice Pudding

Ingredients: *(Time: 3 hours 25 minutes)*

- 1 cup Arborio rice
- 4 cups almond milk
- 1 cup sugar
- Zest of 2 oranges
- ½ cup sliced almonds

Method: *(Servings: 8).*

1. Rinse the Arborio rice under cold water and drain.
2. In the crock pot, combine rice, almond milk, sugar, and orange zest. Stir well.
3. Cover and cook on low for 3 hours, stirring occasionally.
4. In the last 30 minutes, stir in the sliced almonds. Once the rice is creamy and cooked through, turn off the crock pot. 6.Allow it to cool slightly before serving.
5. Serve warm or chilled.

Per serving:

Calories: 162; fat: 5g; carb: 33g; protein: 3g

Almond and Orange Blossom Cake

Ingredients: (Time: 2 hours 55 minutes)

Prep Time: 25 Minutes Cook Time: 2 Hours 30 Minutes Serves: 12 Ingredients:

- 2 cups almond flour
- 1 cup sugar
- 1 teaspoon baking powder
- ½ teaspoon salt
- Zest of 2 oranges
- 4 eggs
- ½ cup olive oil
- ¼ cup orange blossom water

Method: (Servings: 12).

1. In a bowl, combine almond flour, sugar, baking powder, salt, and orange zest.
2. In another bowl, whisk together eggs, olive oil, and orange blossom water.
3. Combine wet and dry ingredients, mixing until well incorporated.
4. Grease the crock pot and pour in the batter. Cover and cook on low for 2.5 hours or until a toothpick comes out clean.
5. Allow the cake to cool before slicing and serving.

Calories: 164; fat: 12g; carb: 11g; protein: 3g

Pistachio and Honey Baklava Bites

Ingredients: *(Time: 2 hours 35 minutes)*

- 1 cup chopped pistachios
- ½ cup honey
- ½ cup unsalted butter, melted
- 1 package phyllo dough, thawed
- Ground cinnamon for dusting

Method: *(Servings: 8).*

1. In a bowl, mix chopped pistachios with honey until well coated.
2. Brush melted butter on the bottom of the crock pot.
3. Place a layer of phyllo dough, brush with butter, and repeat for 4 layers.
4. Spread a third of the pistachio-honey mixture over the phyllo layers.
5. Repeat the layering process, ending with a layer of phyllo on top.
6. Before cooking, cut into bite-sized squares with a sharp knife.
7. Cover and cook on low for 2 hours or until golden brown. Dust with ground cinnamon before serving.

Per serving:

Calories: 123; fat: 8g; carb: 13g; protein: 2g

Lemon Lavender Panna Cotta

Ingredients: *(Time: 6 hours 20 minutes)*

- 2 cups heavy cream

- ½ cup sugar
- Zest of 2 lemons
- 1 tablespoon culinary lavender
- ¼ cup cold water
- 2 ½ teaspoons gelatin
- Fresh berries for garnish

Method: (Servings: 6).

1. In a saucepan, heat the heavy cream and sugar over medium heat until it just begins to simmer. Remove from heat.
2. Add lemon zest and culinary lavender to the cream mixture. Let it steep for 10 minutes, then strain out the zest and lavender.
3. In a small bowl, sprinkle gelatin over cold water. Allow it to bloom for 5 minutes.
4. Add the bloomed gelatin to the warm cream mixture, stirring until fully dissolved.
5. Pour the mixture into the crock pot and cover. Cook on low for 3 hours. After 3 hours, carefully transfer the panna cotta mixture into individual serving glasses or ramekins. Refrigerate for at least 2 hours or until set.
6. Garnish with fresh berries just before serving.

Per serving:

Calories: 186; fat: 15g; carb: 11g; protein: 3g

Chocolate Peanut Clusters

Ingredients: (Time: 2 hours 5 minutes)

- 2 lbs white melting chocolate (white almond bark or candy coating)
- 4 oz. sweet baking chocolate
- 2 cups semi-sweet chocolate chips
- 16 oz. salted dry roasted peanuts
- 8 oz. unsalted dry roasted peanuts

- 8 oz. cocktail peanuts

Method: *(Servings: 20).*

1. Line your kitchen counter with parchment, or 3 baking sheets with parchment.
2. In a large slow cooker, add the white melting chocolate, sweet baking chocolate, and semi-sweet chocolate chips. Put the lid on and set to low for 1-2 hours, stirring occasionally.
3. When the chocolates are all soft and melted enough, stir to combine them.
4. Add all of the nuts to the crock pot and stir them in well. Put the lid on and switch to Warm, or turn off the slow cooker (but leave the crock in the housing to stay warm).
5. Use an ice cream scoop or a Tablespoon, depending on how large you want your peanut clusters, to scoop small mounds onto the parchment paper. After you have used all of the mixture, rinse your crock with hot water.
6. The candies will take about an hour to really set. When they are set, transfer to an air tight container. These keep well for a week or so, and are wonderful to give as gifts.

Per serving:

Calories: 572; fat: 42g; carb: 42g; protein: 16g

Crock Pot Chocolate Cherry Brownies

Ingredients: *(Time: 3 hours 5 minutes)*

- 1 box Brownie mix (unprepared, just the mix)
- 2 cans Cherry pie filling (mine were 21 ounces each)
- 2 sticks butter (unsalted) (2 sticks equals to 1 cup of butter)

Method: *(Servings: 8).*

1. Spray your crock pot with non-stick spray. Add the cherry filling to your crock pot.
2. Melt your butter, and then mix it with the brownie mix in a large bowl.
3. Add the brownie mix and butter mixture on top of the cherries, and cook on high for about 3 hours.
4. Serve with ice cream or whipped cream on top.

Per serving:

Calories: 170; fat: 0.1g; carb: 41g; protein: 0.5g

Peanut Butter Cup Cheesecake

Ingredients: *(Time: 2 hours 45 minutes)*

- 1 ½ cups chocolate cookie crumbs
- ¼ cup unsalted butter, melted
- 16 oz. cream cheese, softened
- 1 cup creamy peanut butter
- 1 cup granulated sugar
- 2 large eggs
- 1 tsp vanilla extract
- 1 cup semisweet chocolate chips
- ¼ cup heavy cream
- Mini peanut butter cups for garnish (optional)

Method: *(Servings: 8).*

1. Grease the inside of the crock pot. In a mixing bowl, combine chocolate cookie crumbs and melted butter. Press the mixture into the bottom of the crock pot to form the crust.

2. In another bowl, beat cream cheese, creamy peanut butter, granulated sugar, eggs, and vanilla extract until smooth. Pour the cream cheese mixture over the crust in the crock pot.
3. Cover and cook on low for 2 hours and 30 minutes, or until the cheesecake is set around the edges but slightly jiggly in the center. Turn off the crock pot and let the cheesecake cool inside with the lid partially open.
4. In a microwave-safe bowl, melt the semisweet chocolate chips with heavy cream, stirring until smooth. Pour the chocolate ganache over the cheesecake and spread it evenly.
5. Refrigerate the cheesecake for a few hours or until the ganache has set. Serve chilled, optionally garnished with mini peanut butter cups.

Per serving:

Calories: 921; fat: 59g; carb: 83g; protein: 24g

Apricot Cobbler

Ingredients: *(Time: 3 hours 15 minutes)*

- 4 cups fresh or canned apricots, sliced
- 1 cup granulated sugar
- 1 cup all-purpose flour
- 2 tsp baking powder
- ¼ tsp salt
- 1 cup milk
- ½ cup unsalted butter, melted
- Vanilla ice cream for serving (optional)

Method: *(Servings: 6).*

1. Grease the inside of the crock pot. Spread the sliced apricots evenly in the crock pot.

2. In a mixing bowl, whisk together granulated sugar, flour, baking powder, and salt.
3. Stir in milk and melted butter until a batter forms.
4. Pour the batter evenly over the apricots in the crock pot.
5. Cover and cook on low for 3 hours, or until the cobbler is set and the top is golden brown. Serve warm, optionally with a scoop of vanilla ice cream.

Per serving:

Calories: 491; fat: 13g; carb: 94g; protein: 7g

Butterscotch Pudding Gingered Pears

Ingredients: (Time: 3 hours 5 minutes)

Prep Time: 35 Minutes Cook Time: 4 Hours Serves: 6 Ingredients:

- ½ cup finely chopped crystallized ginger
- ¼ cup packed brown sugar
- ¼ cup chopped pecans
- 1 ½ teaspoons grated lemon zest
- 6 medium Bartlett or Anjou pears
- 2 tablespoons butter, cubed

Optional:

- Vanilla ice cream and caramel ice cream topping

Method: (Servings: 8).

1. In a small bowl, combine the ginger, brown sugar, pecans and zest.
2. Using a melon baller or long-handled spoon, core pears to within ¼ in. of bottom. Spoon ginger mixture into the center of each pear.
3. Place pears upright in a slow cooker. Top each with butter. Cover and cook on low for 4-5 hours or until tender. If desired, serve with ice cream and caramel topping.

Per serving:

Calories: 217; fat: 7g; carb: 38g; protein: 1.28g

Mocha Pots de Crème

Ingredients: *(Time: 2 hours 15 minutes)*

- 2 cups heavy cream
- 1/2 cup whole milk
- ½ cup granulated sugar
- 2 tsp instant coffee or espresso powder
- 6 oz semisweet chocolate, chopped
- 6 large egg yolks
- 2 tsp vanilla extract
- Whipped cream and chocolate shavings for garnish (optional)

Method: *(Servings: 6).*

1. In a saucepan, combine heavy cream, whole milk, granulated sugar, and instant coffee or espresso powder. Heat over medium heat, stirring until the mixture is hot but not boiling.
2. Remove from heat and add the chopped semisweet chocolate. Stir until the chocolate is melted and the mixture is smooth.
3. In a separate bowl, whisk the egg yolks and vanilla extract.
4. Gradually whisk the chocolate mixture into the egg yolks.
5. Strain the mixture to remove any lumps, then pour it into the crock pot.
6. Cover and cook on low for 2 hours or until the pots de crème are set but slightly wobbly in the center.
7. Let them cool to room temperature, then refrigerate until chilled. 8.Garnish with whipped cream and chocolate shavings if desired.

Per serving:

Calories: 397; fat: 27g, carb: 32g; protein: 5g

Amaretto Cherries with Dumplings

Ingredients: (Time: 8 hours)

- 2 cans (14-1/2 ounces each) pitted tart cherries
- ¾ cup sugar
- ¼ cup corn-starch
- 1/8 teaspoon salt
- ¼ cup amaretto or 1/2 teaspoon almond extract
- 1 cup all-purpose flour
- ¼ cup sugar
- 1 teaspoon baking powder
- ½ teaspoon grated lemon zest
- 1/8 teaspoon salt
- 1/3 cup 2% milk
- 3 tablespoons butter, melted
- Vanilla ice cream, optional

Method: (Servings: 6).

1. Drain cherries, reserving ¼ cup juice. Place cherries in a slow cooker.
2. In a small bowl, mix sugar, cornstarch and salt; stir in reserved juice until smooth. Stir into cherries. Cook, covered, on high for 7 hours.
3. Drizzle amaretto over cherry mixture.
4. For dumplings, in a small bowl, whisk flour, sugar, baking powder, lemon zest and salt. In another bowl, whisk milk and melted butter. Add to flour mixture; stir just until moistened.
5. Drop by tablespoonfuls on top of hot cherry mixture. Cook, covered, 45 minutes or until a toothpick inserted in center of dumplings comes out clean. If desired, serve warm, with ice cream.

Poached Figs

Ingredients: (Time: 5 hours 2 minutes)

- 1⁄2 cup water
- 1⁄2 cup apple juice
- 2 teaspoons honey
- 2 teaspoons sugar
- 1 vanilla bean, split
- 8 ounces' fresh figs

Method: (Servings: 4).

1. In a small saucepan over medium heat, combine the water, apple juice, honey, sugar, and vanilla bean.
2. Heat through until hot but not boiling, about 5 minutes.
3. Place the figs into a 2-quart slow cooker. Pour hot water/apple juice mixture over them.
4. Cook on low for 5 hours or until the figs are cooked through and starting to split.
5. Remove the figs from the poaching liquid and serve.

Per serving:

Calories: 74, fat: 0g, carbs: 19g, protein: 0.5g

Challah Bread Pudding

Ingredients: (Time: 5 hours 15 minutes)

- 4 cups cubed challah 1⁄3 cup dried tart cherries

- 2 1/3 cups fat-free evaporated milk
- 2 large eggs
- 1/3 cup packed dark brown sugar
- 1 teaspoon vanilla extract
- 1 teaspoon cinnamon
- 1/2 teaspoon ground ginger
- 1/4 teaspoon nutmeg

Method: *(Servings: 10).*

1. Spray a 4- to 5-quart slow cooker with cooking spray
2. Add the bread cubes and dried cherries. Stir.
3. In a medium bowl, whisk the evaporated milk, eggs, brown sugar, vanilla, cinnamon, ginger, and nutmeg.
4. Pour over the bread crumbs and dried fruit.
5. Cook for 5 hours on low or until the pudding no longer looks liquid.

Per serving:

Calories: 200, fat: 4g, carbs: 28g, protein: 8g

Orange-Scented Custard

Ingredients: *(Time: 8 hours 10 minutes)*

- 1 tablespoon orange blossom water, or 1/2 teaspoon orange extract
- 2 cups fat-free evaporated milk
- 5 large eggs
- 1/3 cup sugar

Method: *(Servings: 10).*

1. Place all ingredients into a large bowl. Whisk until smooth.
2. Pour into a 4- to 5-quart slow cooker.

3. Cook on low for 8 hours, or until the center looks set and does not jiggle.

Per serving:

Calories: 129, Fat: 4g, Carbs: 12g, Protein: 6.5g

Conclusion

One of the best things about the Mediterranean diet is that it's not as restrictive as other diet programs. It was designed to help you eat clean, tasty food, prepared in the healthiest way there possibly is. When the fresh Mediterranean food is combined with slow cooking, it results into an entirely new dimension of benefits and flavors. Once you start exploring this perfect combination, you can begin enjoying its numerous benefits.

The Mediterranean diet is one of the best scientifically proven eating plans with multiple health benefits. It has been found that following the Mediterranean diet reduces the risk of heart-related diseases, reduces weight, controls blood sugar levels, and reduces stress and depression.

Cooking your meals in a crock pot increase Mediterranean health benefit. The crock pot is one of the biggest innovations when it comes to cooking the healthy way. By cooking your food in the crock pot, you will not lose the flavor or the nutritional value of the food. Slow cooking reduces the destruction and the loss of important nutrients, especially vitamins. Not only that your food will be healthier, but this also means a better taste. And if you're a fanatic, you will always choose fresh ingredients instead of frozen. These are healthier, tastier, and easier to handle in your slow cooker.

Also, the biggest secret of slow cooking is time. This might seems confusing to most people but cooking with a crock pot will not affect your daily activities. This is because we run busy schedules and we simply do not have an entire day to waste with a pot, but we can have a good, tasty, and nourishing dinner. And this is a benefit your crock pot comes with. It is a perfect appliance designed to make your life simple and your dinner healthy and tasty. You can easily prepare your ingredients the day before, throw them in your crock pot, and set the heat to low. The cooker will need all day but you will have a nice dinner at the end of a day.

Therefore, healthy eating isn't just about the ingredients. It's also about the experience. Take time to slow down at dinnertime, rather than just rushing through it. Set a table, to encourage relaxation, pour a glass of wine, and purposefully enjoy a slow meal. Doing so allows the brain to process fullness levels, so overeating is significantly reduced, and stress hormones are minimized when relaxation at mealtime is mindfully approached.

Appendix: Conversions & Equivalents

Volume Equivalents (Liquid)		
Standard	**Us Standard (Ounces)**	**Metric (Approximate)**
2 tablespoons	1 fl. oz.	30 mL
¼ cup	2 fl. oz.	60 mL
½ cup	4 fl. oz.	120 mL
1 cup	8 fl. oz.	240 mL
1½ cups	12 fl. oz.	355 mL
2 cups or 1 pint	16 fl. oz.	475 mL
4 cups or 1 quart	32 fl. oz.	1 L
1 gallon	128 fl.	oz. 4 L

Oven Temperatures	
Fahrenheit (F)	**Celsius (C) (Approximate)**
250°	120°
300°	150°
325°	165°
350°	180°
375°	190°
400°	200°
425°	220°
450°	230°

Volume Equivalents (Dry)	
Standard	**Metric (Approximate)**
⅛ teaspoon	0.5 mL
¼ teaspoon	1 mL
½ teaspoon	2 mL
¾ teaspoon	4 mL
1 teaspoon	5 mL
1 tablespoon	15 mL
¼ cup	59 mL
⅓ cup	79 mL
½ cup	118 mL
⅔ cup	156 mL
¾ cup	177 mL
1 cup	235 mL
2 cups or 1 pint	475 mL
3 cups	700 mL
4 cups or 1 quart	1 L

Weight Equivalents	
Standard	**Metric (Approximate)**
½ ounce	15 g
1 ounce	30 g
2 ounces	60 g
4 ounces	115 g
8 ounces	225 g
12 ounces	340 g
16 ounces or 1 pound	455 g

Appendix 2: Recipe Index

Pork and Sweet Corn Chowder	160
Pork and White Bean Stew	70
Potato Frittata with Cheese and Herbs	40
Potato Vegetable Hash	90
Prussian Cabbage	173
Regal Caper Sauce	184
Rice with Blackened Fish	111
Rice with Pork Chops	112
Ricotta and Parmesan Pancake	41
Rigatoni with Lamb Meatballs	106
Roasted Baby Carrots	94
Roasted Red Pepper and Tomato Soup	61
Rosemary and Pancetta Polenta	42
Rosemary Chicken and Potatoes	149
Rosemary Chicken with Potatoes	141
Rosemary Garlic Mashed Potatoes	171
Rosemary Leg of Lamb	164
Rosemary-Mushroom Sauce	182
Rosemary-Thyme Stew	64
Sausage & Hash Brown Casserole	36
Savory French Toast with Herb Purée	47
Seafood Paella	121
Seafood Stew	119
Sesame-Ginger Cod	132
Shredded Chicken Souvlaki	139
Shrimp and Mushroom Risotto	125
Shrimp Scampi	118
Slow Cooker Beef Curry	161
Slow Cooker Frittata	35
Spanish Saffron Rice	174